Learn SQL Server 7.0 Administration

Jeffrey Garbus

with Alvin Chang and Penny Garbus

Wordware Publishing, Inc.

Library of Congress Cataloging-in-Publication Data

Garbus, Jeffrey
Learn SQL server 7 administration / by Jeffrey Garbus.
p. cm.
Includes index.
ISBN 1-55622-747-7 (pbk.)
1. SQL server. 2. Client/server computing. I. Title.
QA76.9.C55 G37 2000
005.75'85—dc21

00-036469
CIP

2320 Los Rios Boulevard
Plano, Texas 75074

Printed in the United States of America

ISBN 1-55622-747-7

10 9 8 7 6 5 4 3 2 1
0004

All inquiries for volume purchases of this book should be addressed to Wordware Publishing, Inc., at the above address. Telephone inquiries may be made by calling:

(972) 423-0090

Dedication

For my love

J.G.

For my entire family

P.G.

Contents

Introduction xiii

Chapter 1 **Definitions and Concepts** 1
Client/Server Concepts 1
Database Management System (DBMS) 2
SQL Server 2
Systems Administration 2
Database Administration 3
Enterprise Manager 3

Chapter 2 **A Preventive Maintenance Regimen** 7
What Needs to be Maintained? 7
Server-level Maintenance 8
Database-level Maintenance 14
Database Backups 15
Transaction Log Backups 20
DBCC 21
Space Management 23
Database Maintenance Plan Wizard 25
Table-level Maintenance 33
Monitor Growth Changes 34
Update Statistics 34
Table and Index Fragmentation 36
Indexes 36
Index Tuning Wizard 38
Alerts, Jobs, and Operators 39
Your Maintenance Checklist 39

Chapter 3 **Configuration Values** 41
Memory Configuration Options 41
I/O Configuration Options 44
Configuring Server Performance Using Windows NT Options . . . 45
Maximize Throughput 45
Configure Server Tasking 45
Configure Virtual Memory 46

Chapter 4 **Activity Monitoring** 49
Monitoring Tools 49
SQL Enterprise Manager 49
NT Performance Monitor 55

Chapter 5 Monitoring Your Error Log 59
Accessing the Error Log 59
Error Log Messages 61
Severity Level Error Messages 63
Accessing the Application Log 65

Chapter 6 Disaster Recovery Plan 67
What Can Go Wrong? 67
Let's Fix the Problem! 70
Disaster/Remedy Grid 70
Recommended Approach 71

Chapter 7 The Database Consistency Checker (DBCC) 73
DBCC Commands 73
DBCC CHECKALLOC 74
DBCC CHECKCATALOG 76
DBCC CHECKDB 77
DBCC CHECKFILEGROUP 79

Chapter 8 Backing Up and Restoring Your Database 83
Database Backups 83
Backup Types 84
Backup Strategy 85
Backup Approach 87
Standardizing Your Backup Procedures 87
Backing Up the Databases 88
Adding Your Backup Device 93
A Behind-the-Scenes Look: Database Backups 95
Step 1: Back Up the Database 96
Step 2: Back Up the Transaction Log 97
A Behind-the-Scenes Look: Transaction Log Backups 99
The Master Database 100
Restoring Your Database 100
If a Disaster Has Struck 102

Chapter 9 Transaction Log Management 105
Truncating the Transaction Log 105

Chapter 10 Database Space Management 111
Monitoring the Size of Your Database 111

Chapter 11 Updating Index Statistics 117
The Cost-Based Optimizer 117
Commands 118
Update Statistics 119

SP_AUTOSTATS 121
SP_UPDATESTATS 123
DBCC SHOW_STATISTICS 124

Chapter 12 Index Maintenance 127
Rebuilding Your Indexes 127
DBCC DBREINDEX 128

Chapter 13 Alerts, Operators, and Jobs 131
SQL Server Agent 131
Creating New Alerts 133
Creating New Operators 136
Creating New Jobs 138

Appendix A Some Rules to Work By 143
Blocking Problems 143
Blocking Process/Timeout 144
Indexing 145
Indexing/6.5 – 7.0 Upgrade 145
Overallocated Memory 146
Installing SQL Server 147
SQL Server Version 149
Transaction Log is Full 149

Appendix B For Further Information 153

Appendix C The Wizards 155
The Create Database Wizard 156
The Database Maintenance Plan Wizard 160
Specify the Database Backup Plan 163
Specify the Transaction Log Backup Plan 164
The Create Login Wizard 167
The Management Wizards 170
The Backup Wizard 170
The Create Alert Wizard 177

Appendix D Replication 183
Types of Replication 183
Snapshot Replication. 184
Transactional Replication 184
Merge Replication 185
Push vs. Pull 193

Index 199

Acknowledgments

I'd like to thank all of the people whose time and support helped make this possible: Jim Hill at Wordware, for being patient when I told him my late start would not affect the completion date; Alvin and Penny, without whose help this book would not have been completed on time; and my son Brandon for helping reorganize Chapter 6.

Thanks also to Buck Woody, the technical editor, for taking this on and for adding tips from his own considerable experience.

Most of all, I'd like to thank my family, without whose support I might never have slept. Thank you all.

Jeff Garbus

I would like to thank Jeff Garbus for providing me the opportunity to contribute to this book. Thanks to my brother Basil, whose late-night phone calls ran up my phone bill but kept me sane, and thanks to my parents, Yuling and Yuching Chang, who got me started on computers in the first place.

Alvin Chang

I would like to thank Alvin Chang, Buck Woody, Jim Hill, and Jeff Garbus for making this project a professional and enjoyable one.

Penny Garbus

About the Authors

Jeff Garbus

Jeff Garbus's background includes a B.S. degree from Rensselaer Polytechnic Institute, and work experience from PCs to mainframes and back again. He has many years of Microsoft and Sybase SQL Server experience, with a special emphasis on assisting clients in migrating from existing systems to pilot and large-scale projects. He is well known in the industry, having spoken at user conferences and user groups for many years and written articles and columns for many magazines nationally and internationally, as well as having written several books. Recently his focus has been on Very Large Databases, data warehousing, training, and remote database administration.

Jeff has been in consulting for fourteen years, training for nine, and in the software business for eighteen. He has a demonstrated talent for staying at the leading edge of technology, as well as transferring his knowledge to others.

Jeff currently is CEO of Soaring Eagle Consulting, Ltd., an RDBMS consulting and training firm based in Tampa, which specializes in solving business problems as well as performance problems. Soaring Eagle now offers remote database administration services.

He can be reached at jeffg@soaringeagleltd.com.

Alvin Chang

Alvin Chang is a technical trainer, author, and consultant working for Soaring Eagle Consulting, Ltd., a Tampa-based consulting and training firm. A Microsoft Certified Professional for SQL Server, he has taught SQL Server and consulted throughout the United States. Currently specializing in Microsoft and Sybase system administration, Alvin started as a technical trainer for products like Microsoft Office, Lotus Smartsuite, and Lotus Notes before moving into RDBMSs.

He can be reached at alvin@soaringeagleltd.com.

Penny Garbus

Penny Garbus is a technical writer who has been involved in SQL Server training for over five years. She has written several thousand pages of materials on topics including introductory Transact-SQL, systems administration, advanced SQL techniques, and performance and tuning. She has been writing about Microsoft SQL Server since release 6.

Penny is president of Soaring Eagle Consulting, Ltd. She can be reached at Penny@soaringeagleltd.com.

Introduction

Have you suddenly been given responsibility for the maintenance of a Microsoft SQL Server?

There is an abundance of products on the market that use Microsoft SQL Server, and more are on the way every day. There is also a shortage of experienced database administrators (DBAs) on the market. It seems inevitable that some businesses and organizations end up purchasing a sophisticated system that they do not have the staff or background to maintain.

For these organizations, the question becomes: Now that we've got it, what do we need to do to keep it up and running smoothly? There is also an underlying question that we hope does not need to be answered and which we may not voice, in denial: What do we do if something goes wrong?

This book is written for any person who is about to embark upon the task of maintaining a SQL Server. It answers the first question in detail, with the hope that this will prevent needing to answer the second question.

About This Book

Microsoft SQL Server 7.0 is a sophisticated piece of software designed to store and retrieve data. For the latest release, Microsoft has upgraded the server to be as maintenance free as is possible with current technology.

But this does not absolve the systems administrator (SA) or database administrator (DBA) of the responsibility of making sure that the server has the resources it needs in order to function and continue to store data. The best definition this author has ever heard of a great DBA (or SA) is one who you never know is there, because everything is always running smoothly.

This book is geared towards making your SQL Server run as smoothly as it can to make your system as resilient as possible; and in a situation which requires action, teaching you what action to take, based on preparations we'll teach you to make. These teachings are based on the authors' real-life experience, as well as tips and tricks gathered from other experienced production DBAs.

Chapters 1 and 2 of this book discuss basic concepts, and list and describe the tasks you need to perform in order to successfully ensure ongoing system reliability, performance, and preparedness for disaster recovery. The remaining chapters tell you what you are doing and why.

Judging by the definition we've given for a great administrator, you can become a great systems administrator on most small-scale applications by skipping directly to Chapter 3 and reading on from there. If you need clarification, or want an in-depth understanding of a particular subject, simply jump to the chapter that explains that subject in detail.

The only assumptions we make are that you know enough about the hardware to turn the machine on and that you know enough about your environment to use a mouse.

Good luck, and have fun!

Chapter 1

Definitions and Concepts

In this chapter, we introduce some of the concepts that you will be exploring in the balance of this book. This includes client/server computing, the branch of computing that uses Microsoft SQL Server, what Microsoft SQL Server really is (a database engine), and basic systems administration concepts.

Client/Server Concepts

Client/server computing is the branch of computer science in which we try to divide processing into hardware and software modules that may scale and perform their tasks independently. Stated differently, it is the architecture in which client processes (programs run from your PC) request work or data from a server process or processes, which is the SQL Server in your case.

The *client* is the hardware and software combination which shows you data and interfaces with the database. For example, your client workstation may be running Excel, Visual Basic, or a custom application on Windows 95, Windows 98, or Windows 2000 on some Intel- or Celeron-based desktop or laptop computer.

The *server* is the hardware and software combination that runs the database. For example, you might be running Microsoft SQL Server on

Windows 95, Windows 98, Windows NT 4, Windows NT 5, or Windows 2000.

The software you are going to be maintaining is the server software (Microsoft SQL Server) running on your physical server.

Database Management System (DBMS)

A *database management system* is a software program that exists for the purpose of storing and retrieving data. It will deal directly with the operating system to manage disk space, it will keep the users that are accessing the data from modifying the same information at the same time (*lock management* or *transaction management*), and it will guarantee that information that is stored has permanence.

SQL Server

Microsoft SQL Server is a *relational* DBMS (or *RDBMS)*. Relational means that we store the data in *tables*, using *rows* of data, and we relate the information within the tables with *keys*. For example, you may have a table that has a row for each customer (or client or patient). You may have another table that contains invoice information for each billing item for the client. The tables are related together by the customer; the key may be the customer's social security number, or other unique information.

Systems Administration

Systems administration is the task of maintaining the physical environment, trying to ensure stability, and monitoring growth to ensure sufficient resources for the database management system.

Database Administration

Database administration is the task of ensuring the smooth running of the DBMS. This includes running those tasks that ensure good performance, monitoring the changes in the system over time, and everything listed in Chapter 2 of this book.

Enterprise Manager

The Enterprise Manager is a graphical tool used to assist in the tasks of systems administration and database administration. It allows the database to be controlled and maintained from a single, consistent, easy-to-use interface. It has features that are used in the development and modification of databases and their designs. This includes but is not limited to the development and modification of the database tables. The Enterprise Manager also contains helpful wizards to assist in the development of a maintenance schedule to keep a database running smoothly. These maintenance schedules are a series of database and system administration tasks that are run periodically to ensure that the database will run reliably. These maintenance tasks will be discussed in upcoming chapters.

The Enterprise Manager can be found under the Start menu under Microsoft SQL Server 7.0.

1. Click the **Start** button.
2. Click on **Programs**.
3. Select **Microsoft SQL Server 7.0**.
4. Select **Enterprise Manager**.

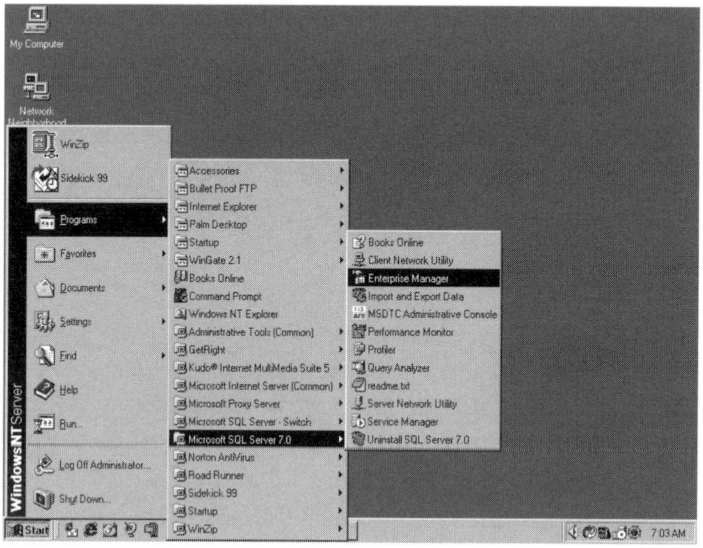

The Enterprise Manager contains lists of SQL Servers including older versions of SQL Server if they are still available and running. Access to most of the configurable items will be displayed in the tree on the left side of the screen.

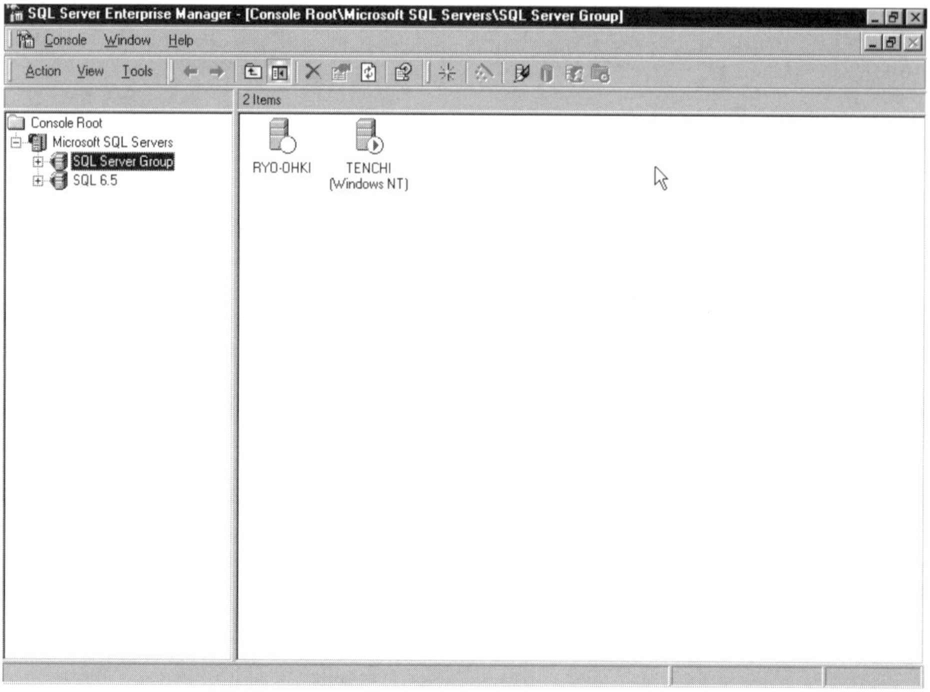

To access the servers click the plus sign (+) beside SQL Server Group to expand it. On the right side of the screen, you will find the taskpad that contains access to many of the necessary administration tasks.

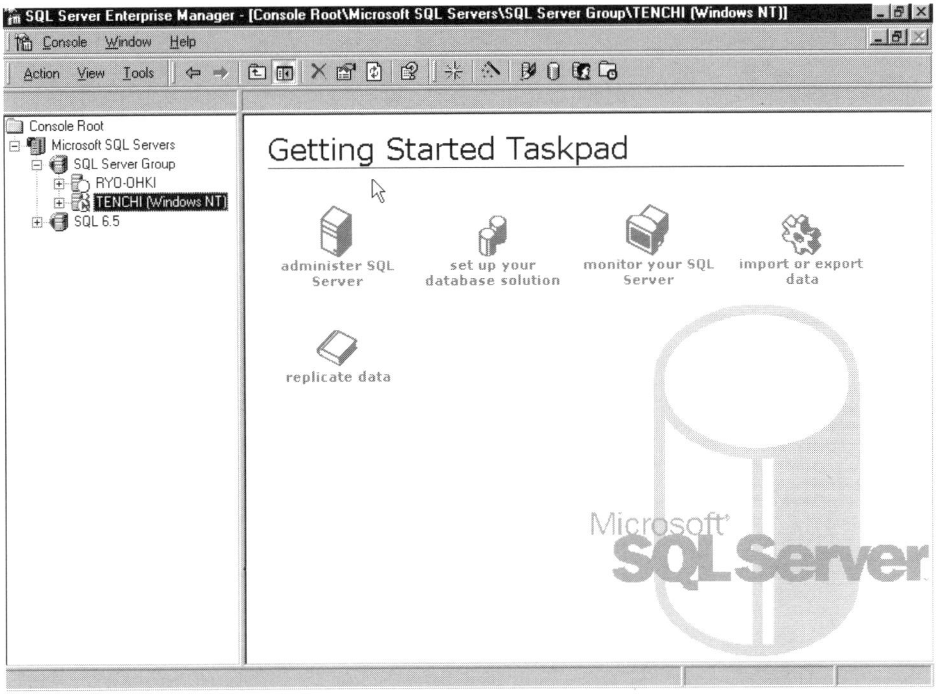

Now that we have discussed the basic concepts and definitions we need, let's move on to putting them into practice. The next chapter introduces the set of tasks you need to perform to keep your system up and running.

Chapter 2

A Preventive Maintenance Regimen

In this chapter, we begin to look at the focus of this book. We will talk about what needs to be maintained, and what you need to do to maintain it. At the end of this chapter, you will find a checklist of recommended tasks categorized by how often they should be performed. Later chapters will look at the importance and frequency of various maintenance tasks in greater detail.

What Needs to be Maintained?

We break down the list of tasks to be performed based on scope. Some tasks take place at the server level, meaning that your tasks involve resources which affect the entire server. For example, memory is a shared resource among all the tasks running on a SQL Server. Other tasks take place at the database level. The database is SQL's unit of backup and recovery, so we perform database backups (making a copy of the database) and other types of care and maintenance we'll discuss in a bit. Finally, at the table level (the table is what contains your data), you do things to help ensure database performance; that is, fast access to the data.

We divide tasks at these levels for purposes of comprehension. For a more practical approach to maintenance, at the end of the chapter we will change the order around a bit as we discuss the frequency of the tasks and put together a maintenance schedule.

Server-level Maintenance

The word “server” is used in a variety of ways in literature, from a file server, which manages disks, to a Windows NT Server, which manages your hardware, to the SQL Server, which interfaces with each to manage your data. Here, we focus on the SQL Server.

Part of systems administration is disaster preparedness. Under some circumstances, you may need to reinstall your entire server. Earlier versions of SQL Server required a significant amount of configuration of the memory parameters, but with Microsoft SQL Server 7.0, almost all parameters are set dynamically and automatically by the server. You may override these, and in fact, the vendor from whom you bought your software may have set some of these parameters to take advantage of SQL Server features for its own software. With Microsoft SQL Server 7.0, you do not need to set any of these parameters yourself, and you should not do so without careful consideration and reading of the SQL Server manuals on the topic. What you should do, though, is make a permanent record of these parameters, and stash it somewhere you can find it if you need it in a stressful situation. If you never need it, fine. However, if one day you do need it, you’ll be glad you took the time. This is a one-time action. To find the current configuration values, use Enterprise Manager like this:

1. Click on the appropriate server name.
2. Click on **Tools** on the menu bar.
3. Click on **SQL Server Configuration Properties**.

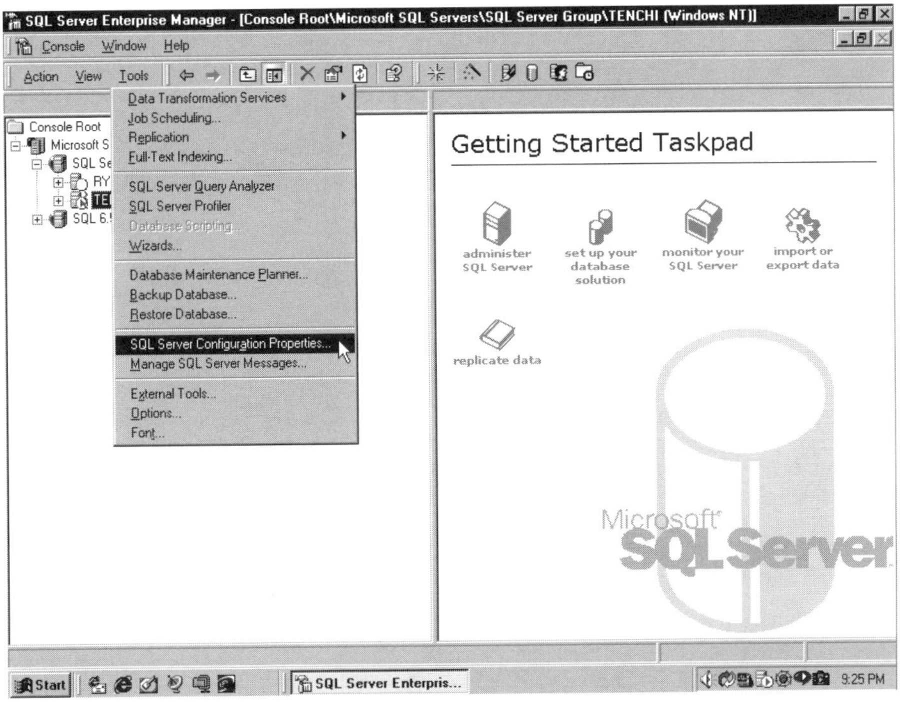

Then click on the appropriate tab and make modifications as shown in the following figures. We recommend you set the SQL Server to start automatically when the operating system is rebooted.

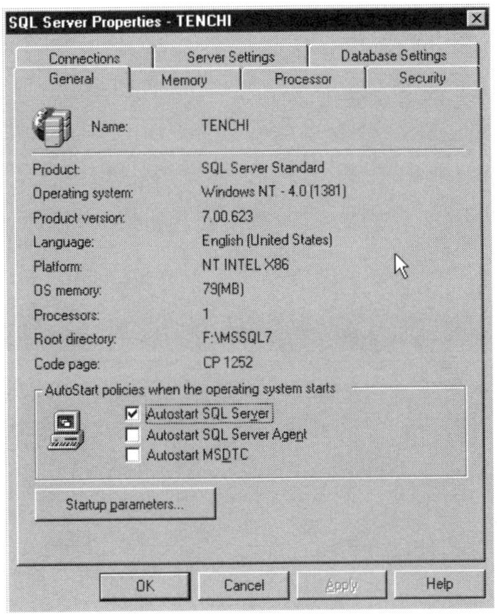

Allow the SQL Server to dynamically allocate memory to make use of any changing server resources.

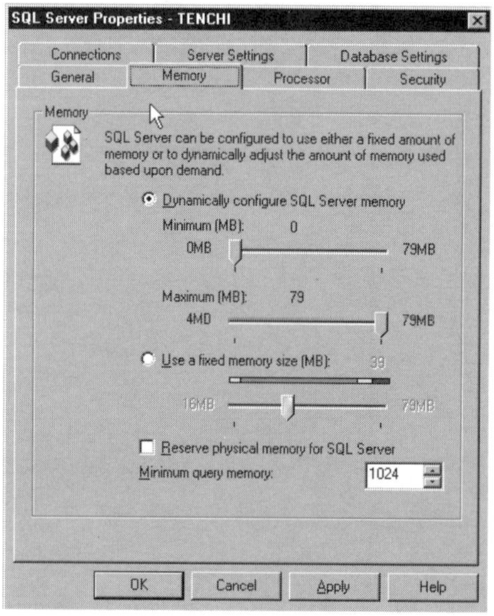

Set the system to use all available processors, unless your application vendor has instructed you otherwise.

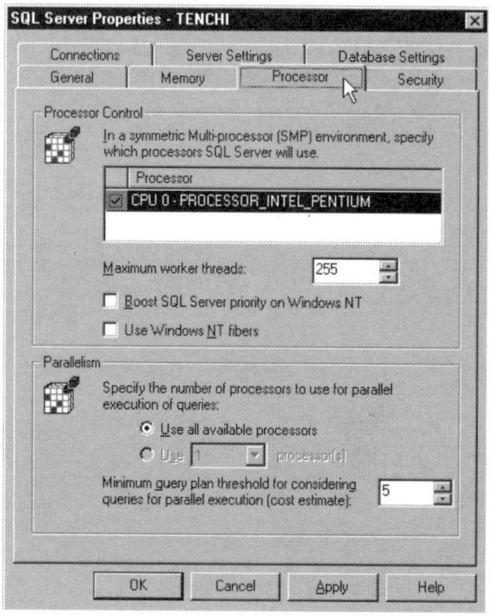

You should leave auditing off unless your site security requires that you track failed attempts at access. You can leave the startup SQL Server account on the default unless you want to change the security from the NT administrator.

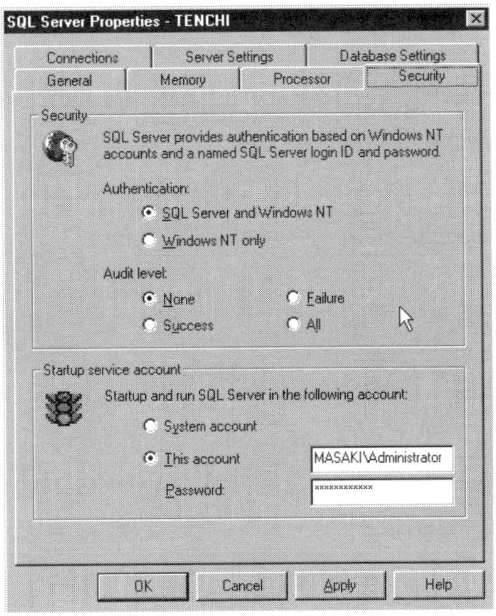

If you have other SQL Servers that need to communicate with this one, make sure the Allow other SQL Servers option is checked. If not, make sure it is unchecked, as you will save a tiny amount of memory resources.

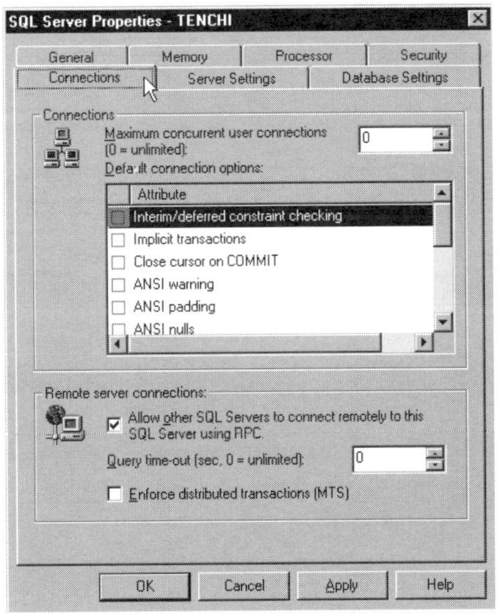

Leave all the defaults on in the Server Settings tab; changing these may affect the behavior of your application in unexpected ways.

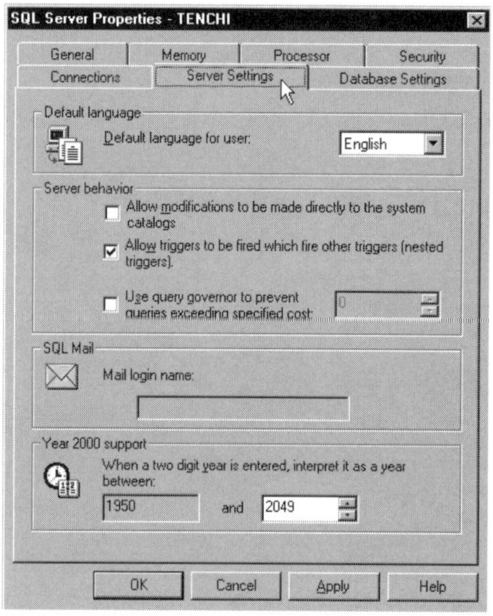

Leave the defaults on in the Database Settings tab as well; this affects administrative tasks, which we will be automating later in this chapter.

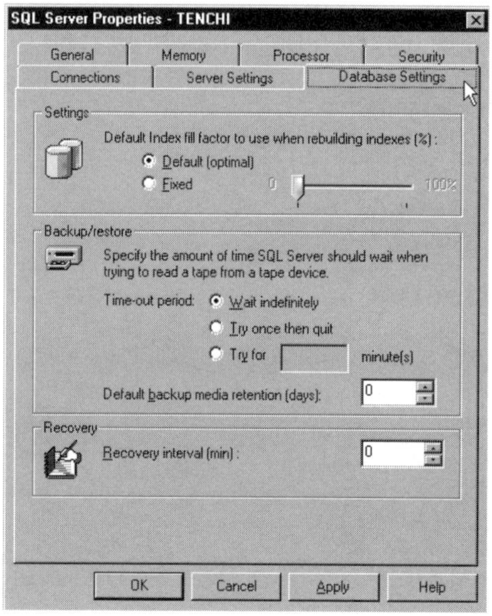

At the server level, you also need to monitor the messages that the server records in the activity log. This will contain information on everything from when the server was started, to warning and error messages of a sufficient severity that the server needs to alert you to them. You can look at the activity log using the following procedure; be sure to do this at least once daily:

1. Open the **Management** folder for the appropriate server.
2. Expand the **SQL Server Logs** item.
3. Click on the appropriate log file.

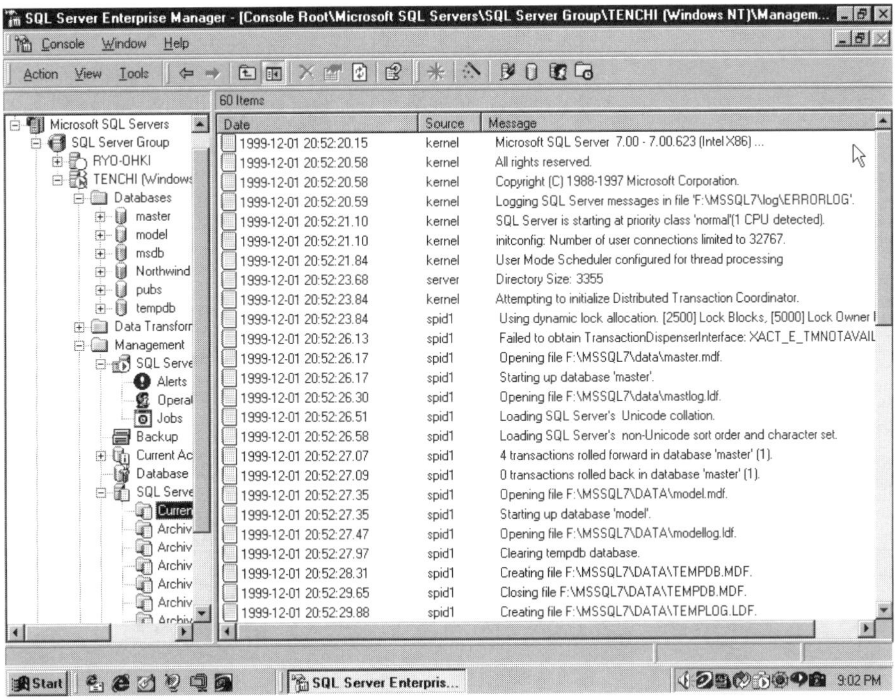

Messages tend to be self-explanatory (they have improved over the years). A low-volume system may rarely get messages other than the standard messages identifying that the server is starting or has started. You should check the log periodically, but at least once a day.

One of the most difficult parts of this job, which requires the most thought and planning, and which you hope is a waste of your time, is to devise a disaster recovery scheme. What happens if somebody steals the machine upon which your server resides? What if a disgruntled employee sets off the automatic sprinkler system, destroying the hardware? What if there is a fire that destroys the hardware? You must give serious consideration to anything that might interrupt your processing, for instance:

- **Loss of Hardware** Plan for a way of getting a new box quickly, if necessary, and a means for loading your server software and database back on it.
- **Loss of Power** A UPS (uninterruptible power supply) is essential; in case of a loss of power, you do not want your server to suddenly shut down. This can cause data loss or database corruption. You can get a UPS from any computer supply shop or, these days, office supply store.
- **Loss of Data** You may experience loss of data for a variety of reasons, largely due to user error. (For example, perhaps somebody accidentally deleted an entire table rather than a single row.) Many shops do not bother to devise a recovery plan at this level, but you should carefully consider the possible consequences of your decision not to.

Database corruption is unusual (you may never experience this), but if it does occur, you must restore the database from your backup. You should always restore a database in its entirety; partial database restorations should be left to seasoned professionals. This is the quickest and most sure route to a functioning SQL Server.

Finally, in the server-level category for Microsoft SQL Server, keep an eye on overall resources. The server will do much of this for you, but it has no idea what to do when you run out of disk space, so plan ahead. Calculate how much space you need for data, figure out when you will need more disk space, and have an extra disk ready in advance.

Database-level Maintenance

Database-level maintenance refers to the tasks we perform on each database as a whole. Note the stress on the word "each"; there is a reason for this. Many sites forget that it is important to maintain every database, not just the production databases. There are also several system databases you need to maintain. Make sure that you pay attention to every database listed in Enterprise Manager. Likewise, every maintenance task is important, and skipping any specific task runs the risk of jeopardizing your production system.

Database Backups

A *database backup* is a copy of all of the used data pages that are stored on disk in the database. The database is the basic unit of recovery for a SQL Server. This means that in case of disaster, you may have to take this backup, replace the current damaged database or database device, and work from that point forward. This is not a situation you want to encounter, but it is an important one for which to prepare.

Note: The phrase *database backup* is used interchangeably with the phrase *database dump*. With the advent of Microsoft SQL Server 7.0, Microsoft has changed the terminology (and syntax) from dump to backup. Because our focus is on Microsoft SQL Server 7.0, we will endeavor to use the word backup.

Backing up your database is important, largely because bad things happen at the worst possible time. However, this precaution is not enough; you need to do two more things to guarantee that your backup will be useful in case of a disaster. First, you need to make sure that the backup will actually load. Second, you need to keep a copy of the backup off-site.

Why might the backup fail to load? The most common reason (and unfortunately, this does happen) is a failure in the backup media. For example, a floppy disk, Zip drive, tape, etc., has a physical flaw, which makes the disk unreadable. If this happens, you could end up with a box full of bad tapes and several months' worth of backups that don't work.

Why do we need to get a copy of the backup off-site? This is because some types of disaster are site-specific. Some examples: theft of equipment, flood, fire, hurricane, earthquake, mudslide, automatic sprinkler failure.... We're sure you can think of others. Any of these situations, which can and do occur, will make you glad you can order another physical server, take your backup devices out of the vault, load the SQL Server, and load from your backups.

As far as backups go, you can back up a database at any time. You do not need to wait until your system is inactive. Backups are performed like this:

1. Choose the appropriate database.
2. Click on the **General** tab on the taskpad.

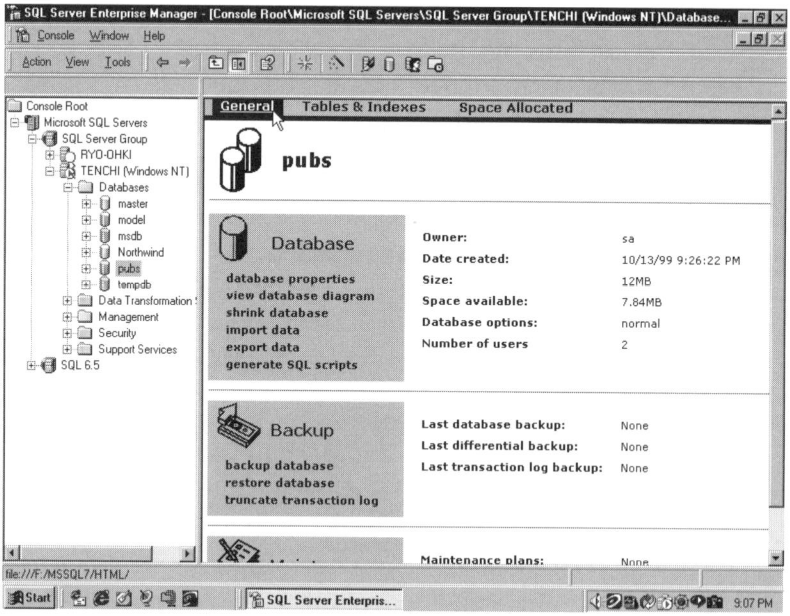

3. Click **backup database.**

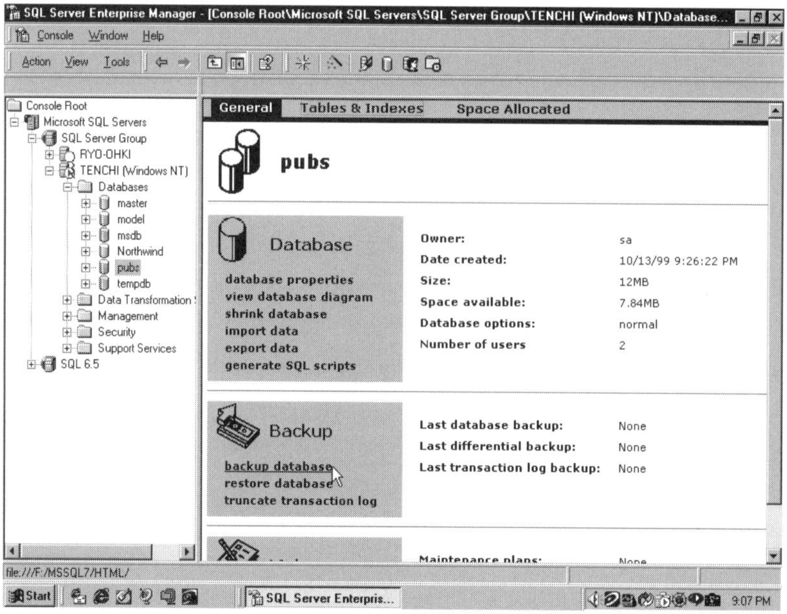

4. Choose the appropriate database from the database list.
5. Type a name for the backup file in the Name box.
6. Select the destination type for the backup. You have a variety of options here, which are explained later in Chapter 8. For now, choose your primary backup storage media and click **OK**.

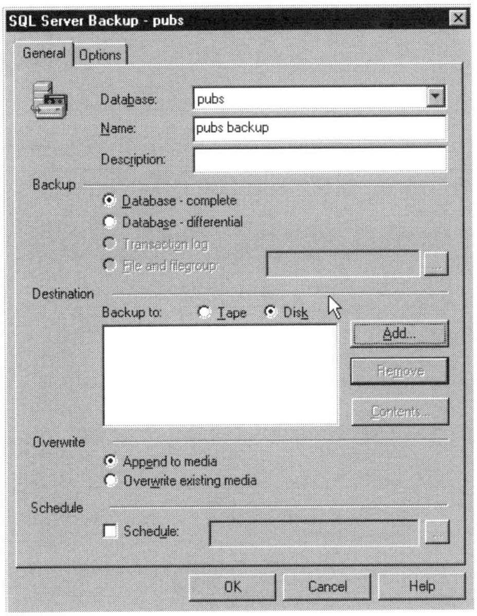

7. In the Choose Backup Destination dialog box, enter the name of the backup file.

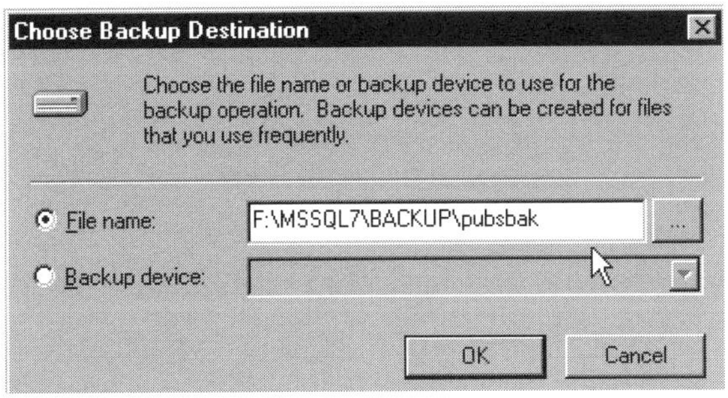

8. Click **OK** to start the backup.

Now that the backup seems successful, try to load the database. If your database was live (in use) when you created the backup, be sure to load to a database other than your live production database (for example, if you backed up *accounting_prime* you should load to something like *accounting_test*).

You can test your backup by restoring it like this:

1. Click on the Tools menu.
2. Select **Restore Database**.
3. Enter the name of the database to be restored (since the original is still here we will have to name it something different).

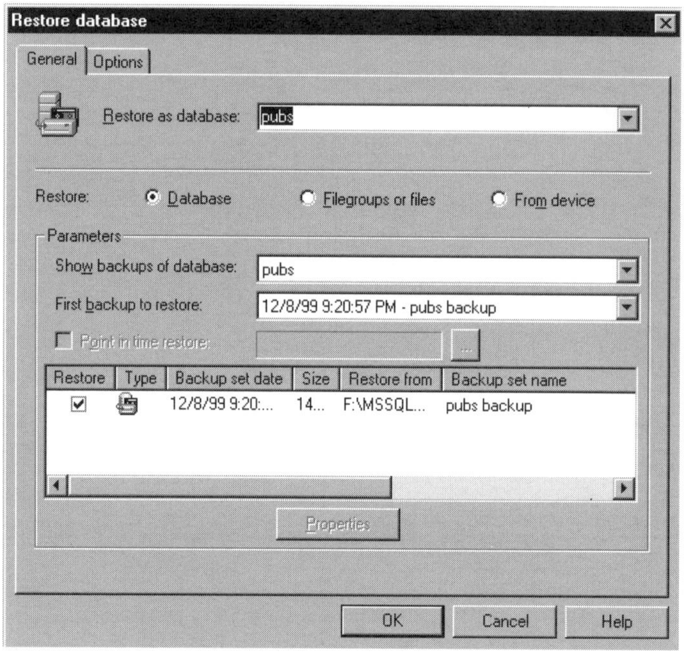

4. Select the name of the database that was backed up from the Show backups of database box.
5. Now select the database backup that was just made from the set of provided backups by checking the appropriate box in the Restore column.

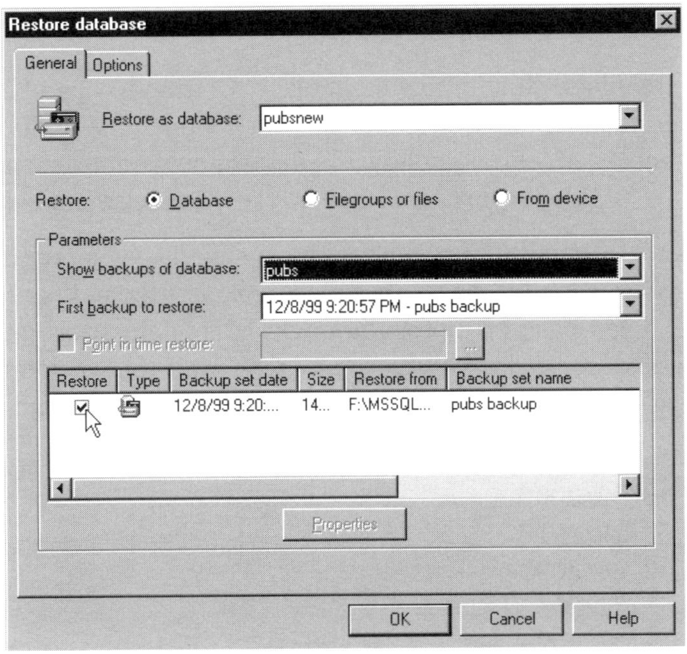

6. Click the **Options** tab and make sure the database files are being restored to the appropriate location.

Note: Because our original database still exists, we need to make sure we do not inadvertently overlay information we care about; once a database is loaded, the old one is erased. This is normally done automatically by Enterprise Manager, but DBAs tend to spell things out for safety's sake.

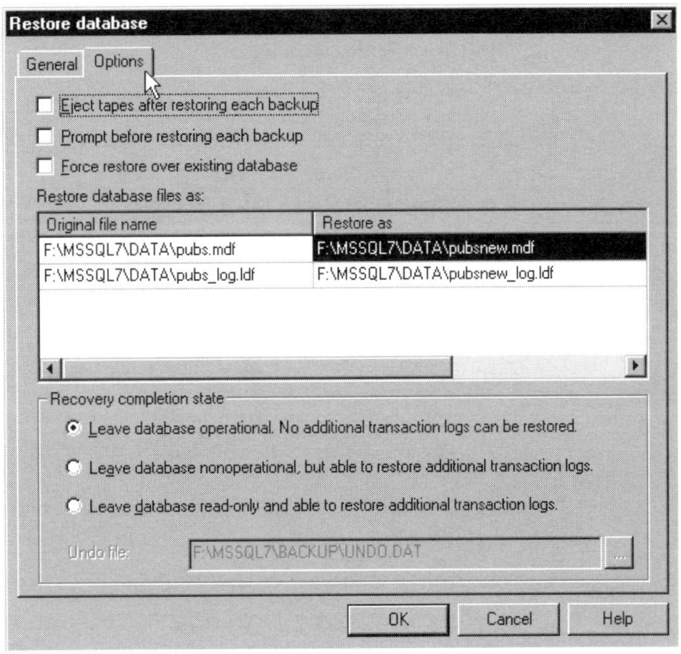

7. Click **OK** to start the restoration.

The new database should now be in place. Getting a copy off-site will depend on the security restrictions of your particular site. Check with a decision-maker at your company and determine whether it should go into a vault, safety deposit box, or a shoe box in your bedroom closet.

The process of reusing your backup storage media (whether it be floppies, tapes, Zip disks, or Jaz drives) is called *aging out* the old media. For example, if you have 10 tapes, you might make daily backups, and transfer the whole week's backups onto one tape after the week is up. For example, if today is 3/30/2000, your tapes might correspond with these dates:

Tape 1: 3/30/2000
Tape 2: 3/29/2000
Tape 3: 3/28/2000
Tape 4: 3/27/2000
Tape 5: 3/26/2000
Tape 6: 3/25/2000
Tape 7: 3/24/2000
Tape 8: 3/17/2000
Tape 9: 3/10/2000
Tape 10: 3/03/2000

The idea is to pick a pivotal date, keep some backups for a period of time, and age them out as your business rules/policies deem them useless.

Transaction Log Backups

A database management system is transactionally based. This means that any specific action you take, from adding a new customer to marking an invoice paid, needs to finish completely. You do not want, for example, your money account to be updated with a paid invoice, but have the invoice left marked unpaid due to a sudden power outage. This leads to unhappy customers and a lot of work by your bookkeepers.

To avoid this, the Microsoft SQL Server keeps a transaction log of all changes to the database, as well as whether multiple modifications belong together in a single transaction. This transaction log will grow until it is truncated, unless you have the database option Truncate log on checkpoint turned on. Which is best for you? If your application needs up-to-the-second recovery, use transaction logging, and do not use the database option. If you do not have the resources to back up the transaction logs, then turn the option on, because otherwise your server will stop processing new transactions when the log fills up. You back up your transaction logs like this:

1. Choose the appropriate database.
2. Select **backup database**.
3. On the General tab, select **Transaction log** under Backup.

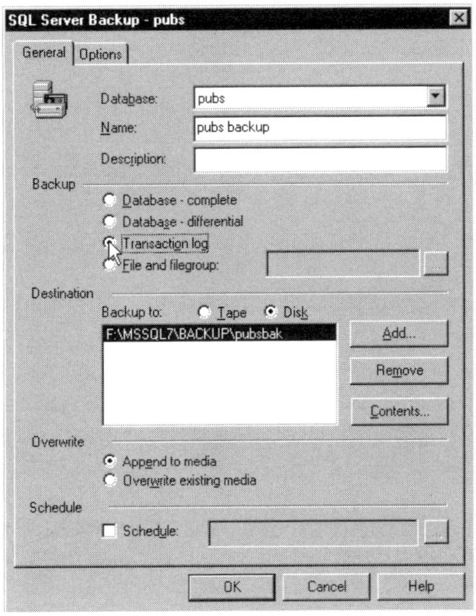

Add a new device if necessary (you may also choose to append the backup to any existing files).

DBCC

The Database Consistency Checker (DBCC) is a tool that verifies the integrity of your database. The tables and indexes on your system reside on disk in complex structures that are fine most of the time. You may run for years without a problem, but on the off chance that a problem shows up, it is better to identify it with DBCC, which may repair the problem, than to find out about it when a query fails.

For each database, you have to run the following:

- DBCC CHECKCATALOG
- DBCC CHECKDB

DBCCs are performed using the Query Analyzer:

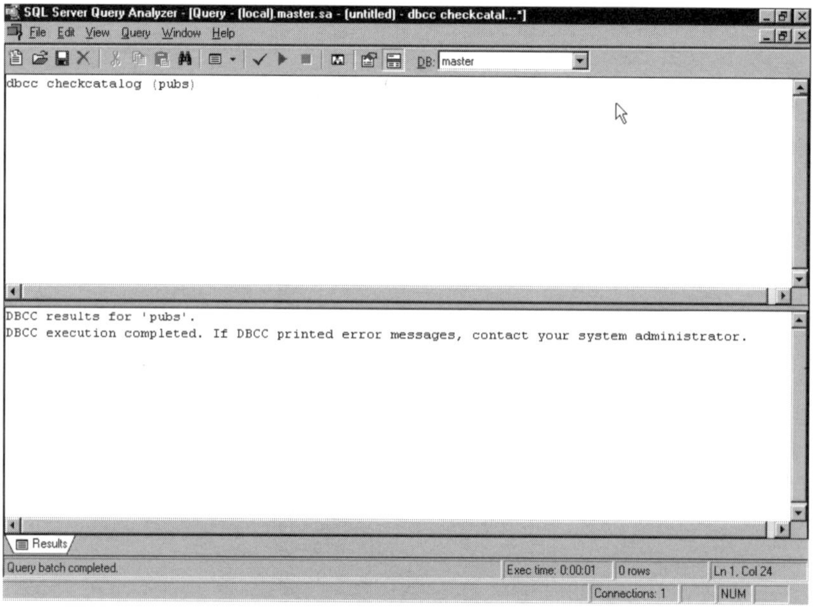

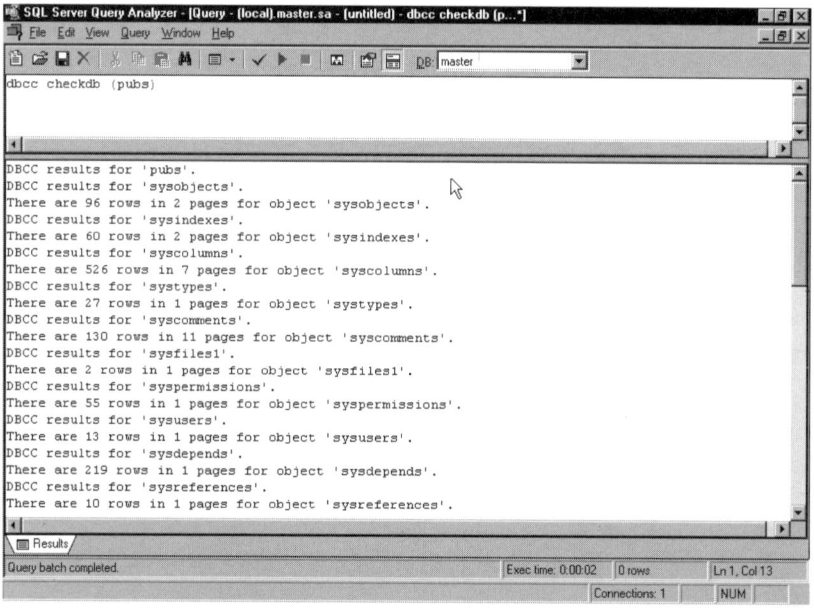

Ideally, you should run DBCCs before you back up your database. The most important thing to consider is that you should be sure you run DBCCs before aging out your backups, because running DBCCs are the only way to guarantee that the data you are storing is going to be of value when you choose to load it.

Space Management

On a SQL Server, disk space is set aside (allocated) immediately when the database is created. You need to make sure of two things: First, make sure too much space isn't allocated. It unnecessarily uses up your disk resources, and slows down your database loads (it won't slow down the backups because the server only backs up used data pages). Secondly, and of more importance, you need to make sure that you have sufficient room for the database to grow. Microsoft SQL Server has an auto-grow (and auto-shrink) option with database creation. This gives you the ability to instruct the database to shrink to a size that makes backups and restorations as quick as possible, and to grow automatically when extra disk space is needed. All you have to do is tell the server where to go for the extra disk space.

First, you determine how much space you have allocated, and how much is in use by selecting Space Allocated from the taskpad for the appropriate database.

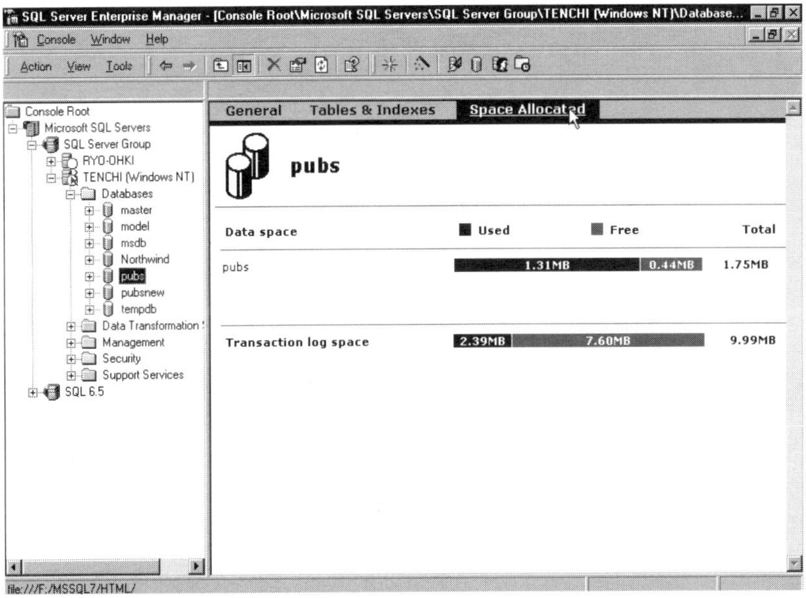

To set your database up for auto-grow/auto-shrink:

1. Right-click the database and select **Properties** from the menu.

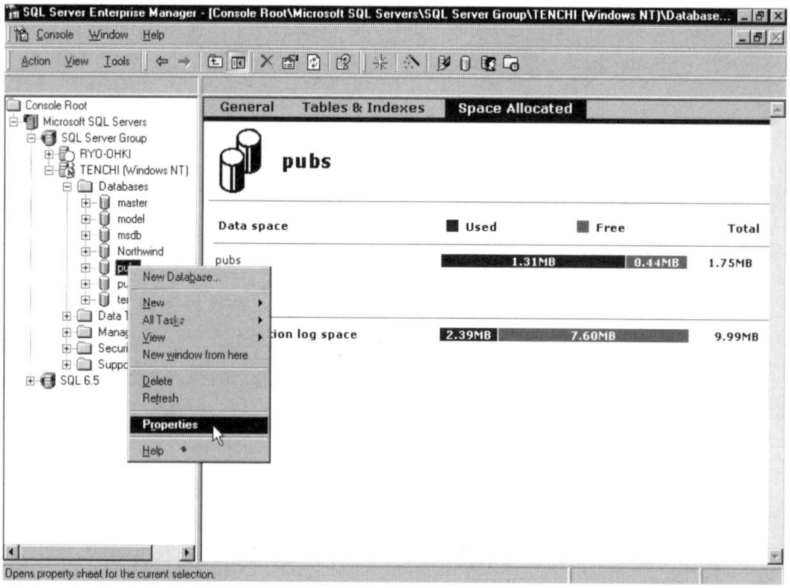

2. Select the appropriate file from the list of database files. Check **Automatically grow file** in the dialog box. (This option also exists on the Transaction Log tab so transaction log files can also be set to auto-grow.)

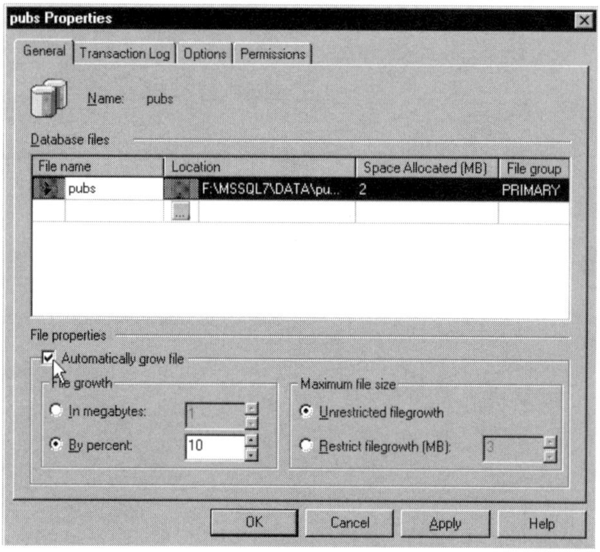

3. Click the **Options** tab.
4. Check **Auto shrink** to enable the option.
5. Click **OK** to set the options.

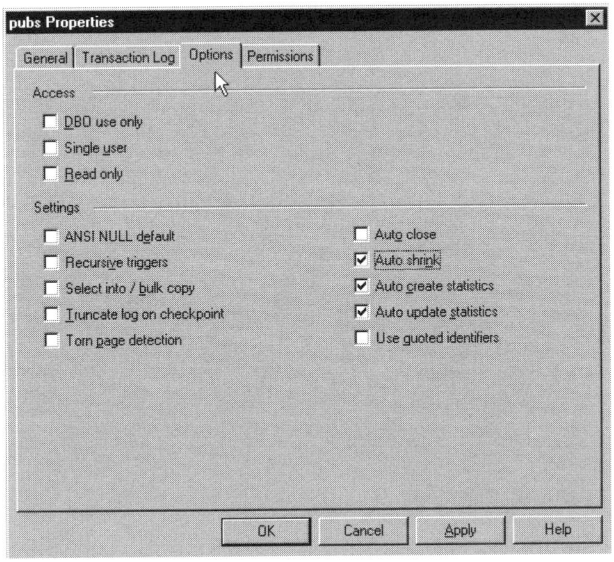

You should monitor the space growth of your database(s). It is a good idea to check the allocated space once a week, every week, and chart the growth.

Database Maintenance Plan Wizard

You can use the Database Maintenance Plan Wizard to automate many of the database-level tasks we've described. You can find this by looking at the bottom of your Console Root tree, and clicking on Database Maintenance Plans.

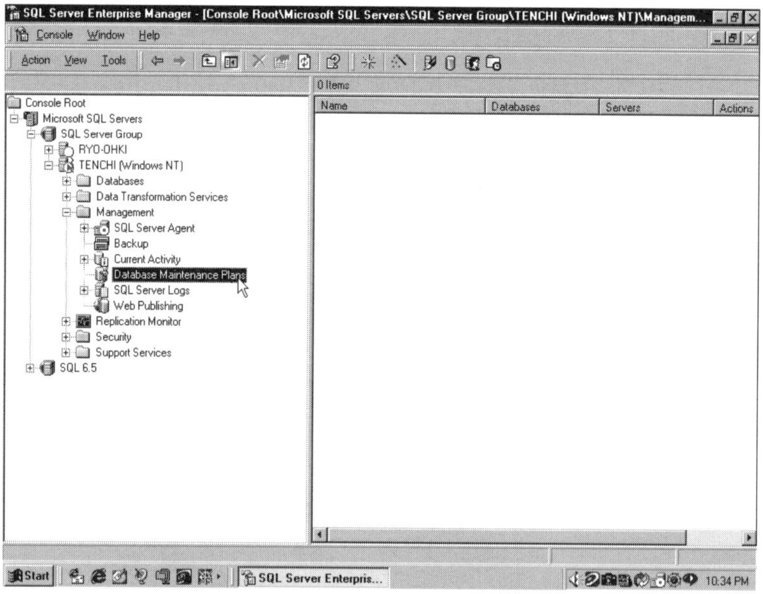

To create a new plan:

1. Right-click on **Database Maintenance Plans** and select **New Maintenance Plan**.

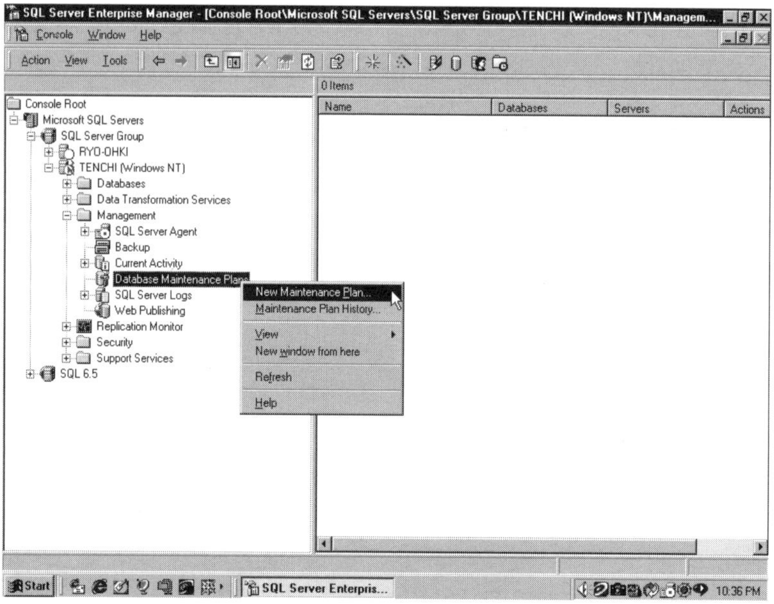

The wizard opens:

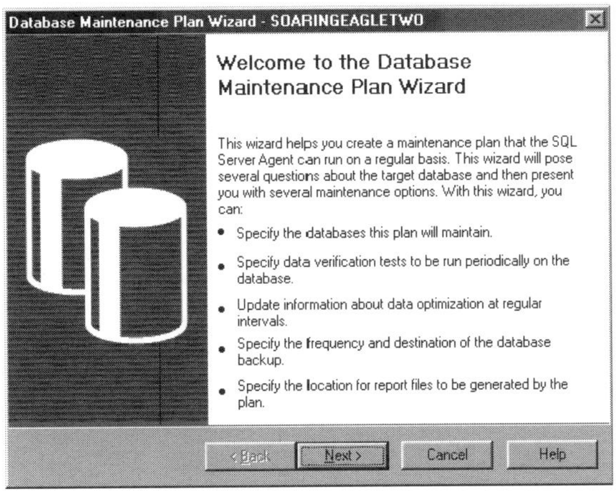

2. Click **Next**. Choose the database for which you want to create a maintenance plan, and click **Next**.

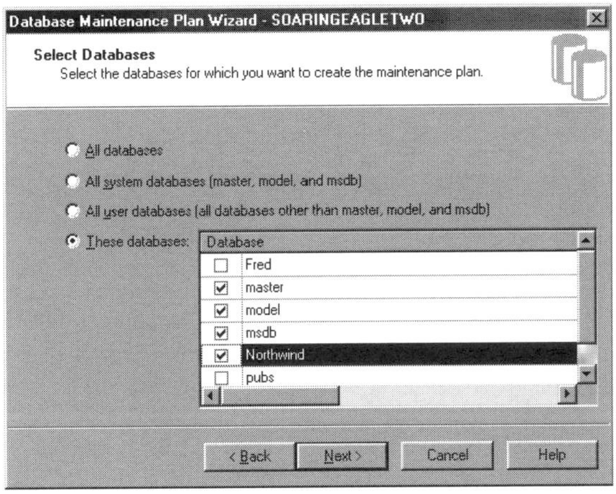

3. Decide on the appropriate schedule for your databases.

Note: We recommend that you do all the system databases together (master, model, and msdb), and your user databases separately. Don't be shy about letting the server do all the work listed, and about checking all the boxes you see. In fact, we recommend you check the box labeled All databases. That way, you will even maintain newly created databases. Otherwise, you will need an additional plan each time you add an additional database.

4. If you want to modify the schedule, click **Change** to open the Edit Schedule dialog box.

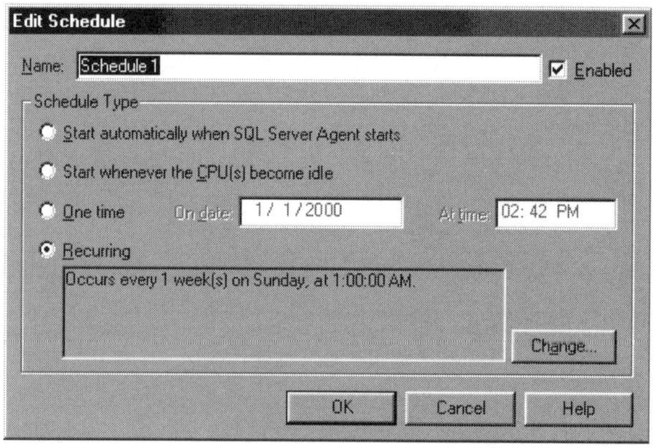

5. Click **Change** again to open the Edit Recurring Job Schedule dialog box and specify your desired frequency. If you clicked anything other than Recurring under Schedule Type in step 4, this dialog box will not be opened.

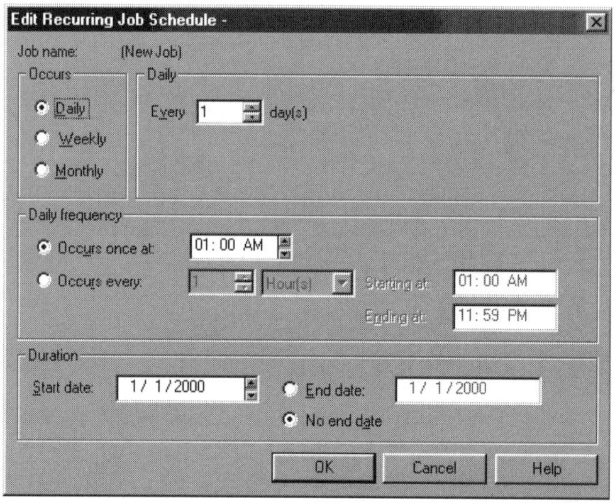

6. Click **OK** followed by **Next** to continue with the wizard.

Note: We recommend backing up all of your databases every night, so we're making it part of the maintenance plan. Make sure you have enough space to back up your databases on your target devices. If not, the backup will not complete, and you will be at risk for data loss.

7. In the Run Data Integrity Tests dialog box, check all appropriate boxes; here, we've chosen to run integrity tests to check the data and the system tables.

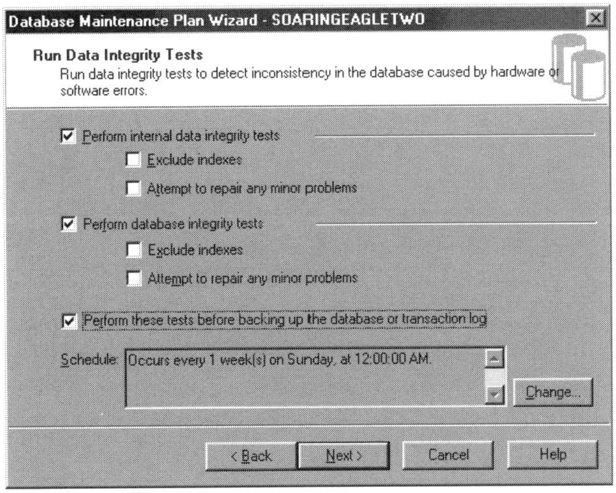

8. Specify backup frequency. (This says every week, but we recommend daily.) Clicking on the Change button will allow you to set a different schedule for database backups.

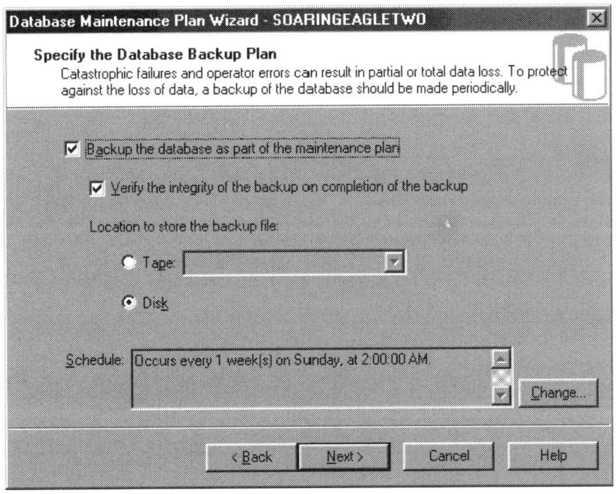

9. Click **Next**. This screen allows you to determine how the backups will be stored on disk. By default, SQL Server will place all backup files in its own backup directory. This can be changed if necessary by changing the Use this directory option and entering a new location in the box.

If the Create a subdirectory for each database option is checked, SQL Server will separate backups for different databases by automatically putting the files in separate directories. If you don't want to keep the backups permanently, the Remove files older than option can be changed so that backup files of a certain age will automatically be deleted.

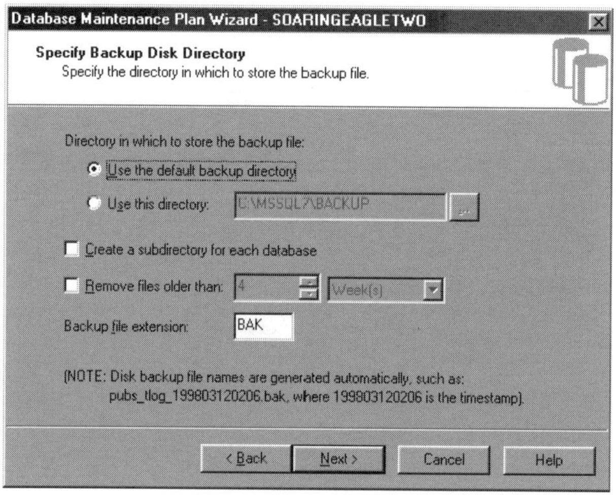

10. Click **Next**. We recommend backing up the transaction log as well; remember, this cleans out the log and keeps its size manageable. Most of the options for transaction log backups are the same as database backups, but they may need to be scheduled more frequently and must work in conjunction with a full database backup.

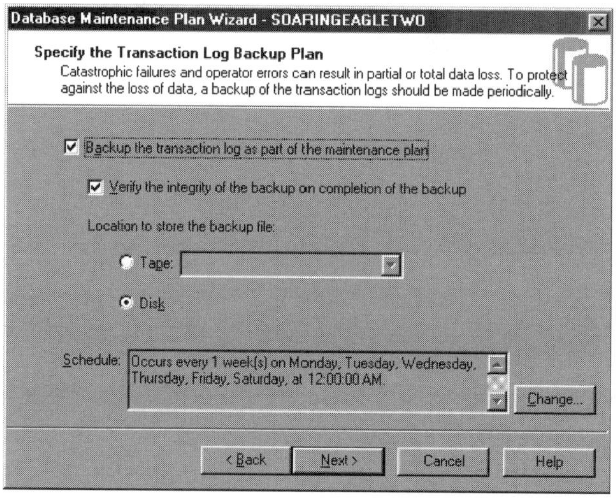

11. Click **Next**. This screen allows you to set the same types of file options for a transaction log backup as a database backup. Make sure your target directory has sufficient space before you decide to use it.

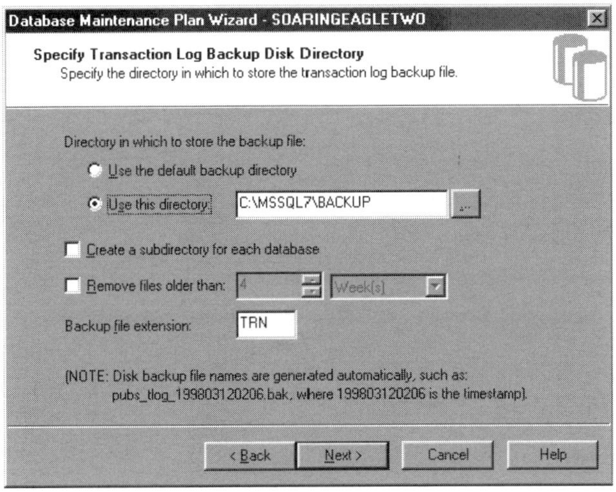

12. Click **Next**. You do want reports written, to either a text file or HTML, depending on where it will be easiest for you to check it.

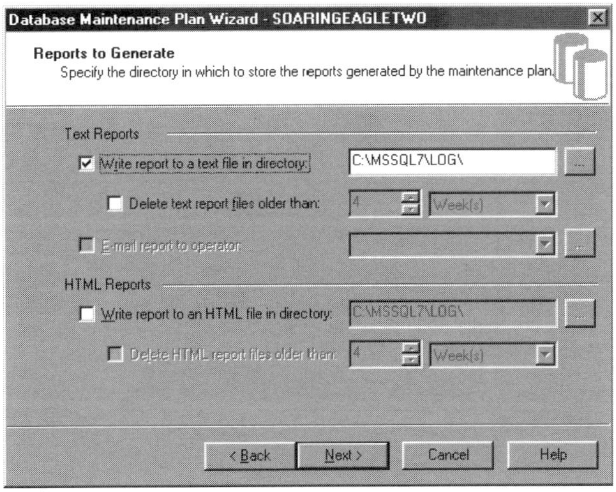

13. Click **Next**. The plan records its actions in a database table. If the table is stored on a different server, you should specify the remote server on which the history will be stored, Otherwise, choose the default and store the history in its own server.

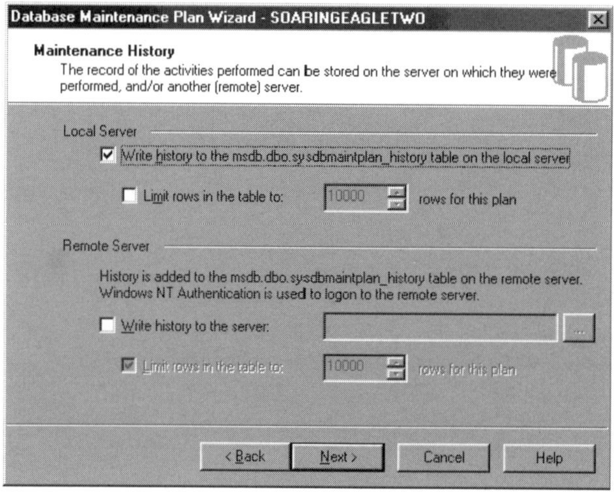

14. Click **Next**. Here you can name your plan.

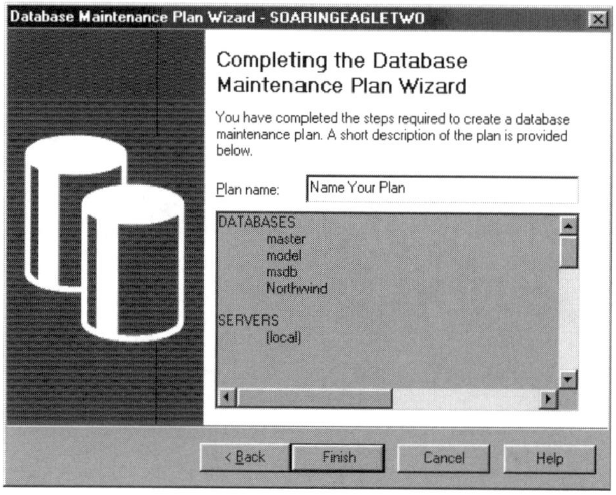

15. Click **Finish** to display your plan in the Enterprise Manager window.

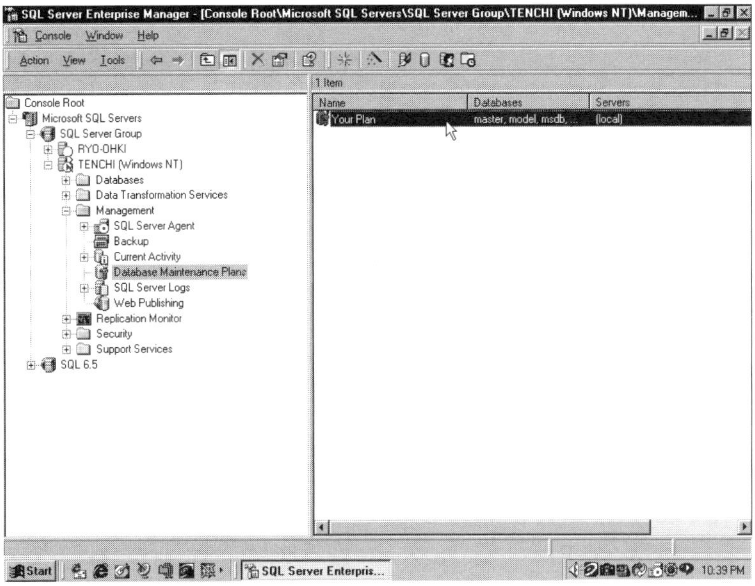

One final note: If it looks like your plan is not running, make sure the Agent is running; this is a requirement for the plans to execute. (The SQL Server Agent is an NT process and is described in Chapter 13.)

Table-level Maintenance

Tables are what contain data in a relational database. When you add a customer to your database, you are actually inserting a row (instance) of data into a table. (You would be amazed at the percentage of databases that have a table named Customer!)

In addition to the tables themselves, the tables usually have other objects that are assigned to them called *indexes*. The purpose of an index is to improve performance of your database. If, for example, you have a million rows in a table, and you want to retrieve one of them, it is not efficient to read all the rows of the table in order to get the row you are looking for. The index dramatically reduces the number of page requests it takes to find the row you want.

Monitor Growth Changes

If you know enough about your data to understand the growth of the individual tables, then you should keep an eye on the growth rates of these individual tables. If not, it may be good enough for you to track the overall database size instead. Sudden growth or shrinkage merits investigation. Also, if any of your tables are especially volatile, keep a close eye on them.

Update Statistics

Microsoft SQL Server has a cost-based optimizer. The optimizer itself is the part of the DBMS which determines the approach the server will use to retrieve your data. *Cost-based* means that the server determines at query time how it will try to retrieve the information you request. In order for the server to estimate which indexes to use, it looks at a *statistics page*. The statistics page contains information that describes to the Microsoft SQL Server how those data are distributed so that it can appropriately match an index to a query. Put another way, if your statistics are up to date, the optimizer is much more likely to pick the best plan for your query, and you will get your results back faster.

Here's the good news: For Microsoft SQL Server 7.0, the updating of statistics is now automatic and happens over the course of the utilization of the table. If your system is older than version 7.0, you will have to update statistics manually and regularly (as often as weekly or daily!). Even though updating statistics over time is automatic, you may need to perform this task manually anyway, as the index's distribution skews ahead of the automatic update process (the distribution may change faster than the automatic update process can keep up). Also, after your initial data load, you may want to update the statistics to give the optimizer a head start. You can update the statistics manually (but this is not something you necessarily need to do very often).

Open the Query Analyzer program:

1. Click the **Start** button.
2. Select **Microsoft SQL Server 7.0**.
3. Select **Query Analyzer**.

To execute the Update Statistics command:

4. Type the command in the query window.
5. Click the **Execute** button (looks like a green Play button).

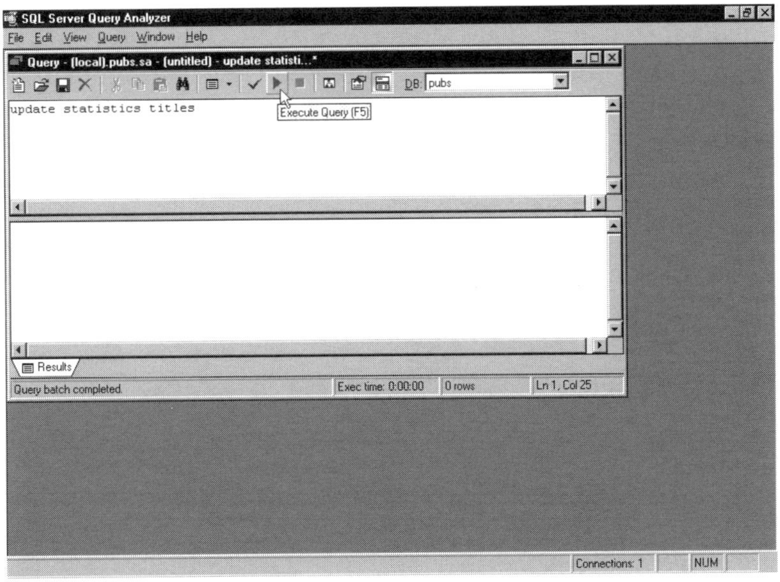

If you want to get a step ahead of your data, you can monitor data distribution changes using sp_statistics, like this:

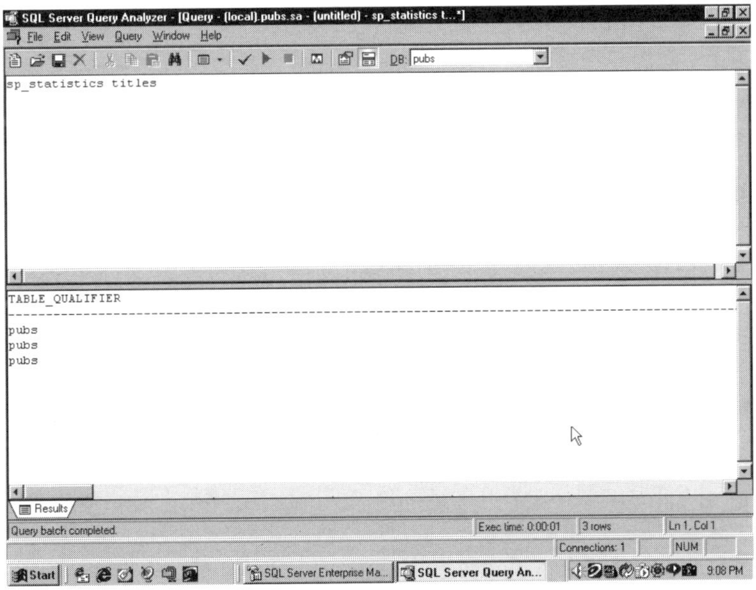

Table and Index Fragmentation

As data is added to your table, removed from your table, updated, and moved around in your table, and index entries are rearranged accordingly, it is possible to get into a situation where your data is poorly organized in storage. More specifically, the pages (the basic physical storage units) that the data are stored on may become underutilized or spread out too far on the disk to be sequentially retrieved optimally. Said another way, sometimes you have to reorganize the way the data are stored on the disk. You can check the level of contiguity using the DBCC showcontig function.

```
DBCC SHOWCONTIG scanning 'authors' table...
[SHOW_CONTIG - SCAN ANALYSIS]
_____________________________________
Table: 'authors' (117575457) Indid: 1 dbid:5
TABLE level scan performed.
- Pages Scanned................................: 2
- Extents Scanned..............................: 2
- Extent Switches..............................: 1
- Avg. Pages per Extent........................: 1.0
- Scan Density [Best Count:Actual Count].......: 50.00% [1:2]
- Logical Scan Fragmentation ..................: 0.00%
- Extent Scan Fragmentation ...................: 50.00%
- Avg. Bytes free per page.....................: 7051.0
- Avg. Page density (full).....................: 12.89%
(11 row(s) affected)
DBCC execution completed. If DBCC printed error messages, contact your
system administrator.
```

This tells you how full the pages are. A page contains 8,192 bytes. (Think of a byte as one character of information.) If your pages are under 50% utilized, you are probably wasting space, and should consider dropping and rebuilding your clustered indexes in order to clean up the data. (We will discuss how to do this in just a moment).

Indexes

Indexes are the physical implementation of performance design for SQL Server tables. The index information is stored on pages just as data are, and can become fragmented in the same way that data do. If an index becomes fragmented, your only option is to drop it and rebuild it.

A shortcut to dropping and rebuilding all indexes for a table, as well as reorganizing the data for the table, is to drop and rebuild the clustered index on the table. Each table in a production database has at most one clustered index. In addition, each table in a production database should have a clustered index. In fact, if you have tables that do not have a clustered index on each table, you should contact the person or organization responsible for the database design and ask for an explanation.

You can drop a clustered index like this:

1. Right-click on a table in the Enterprise Manager.
2. Select **All Tasks**.
3. Select **Manage Indexes**.

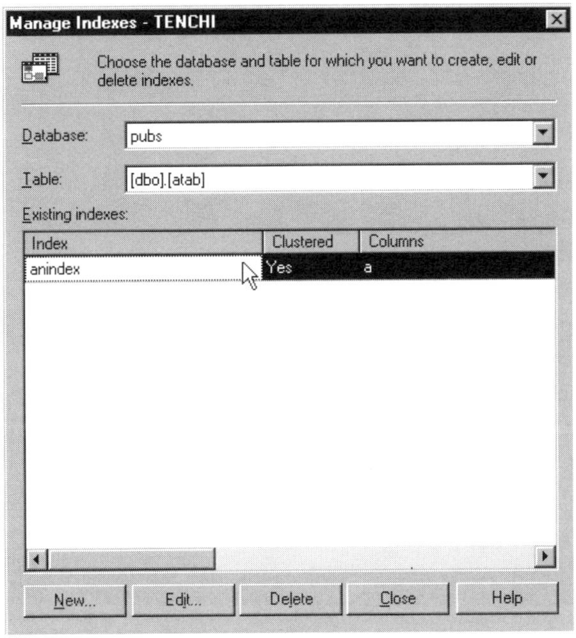

4. Click on the index to be deleted.
5. Click the **Delete** button.

To create a new index:

1. Click the **New** button in the Manage Indexes dialog.
2. Type a unique name for the index in the Index name box.
3. Check the columns to be indexed.
4. Check the Clustered index option if the index is to be a clustered index.

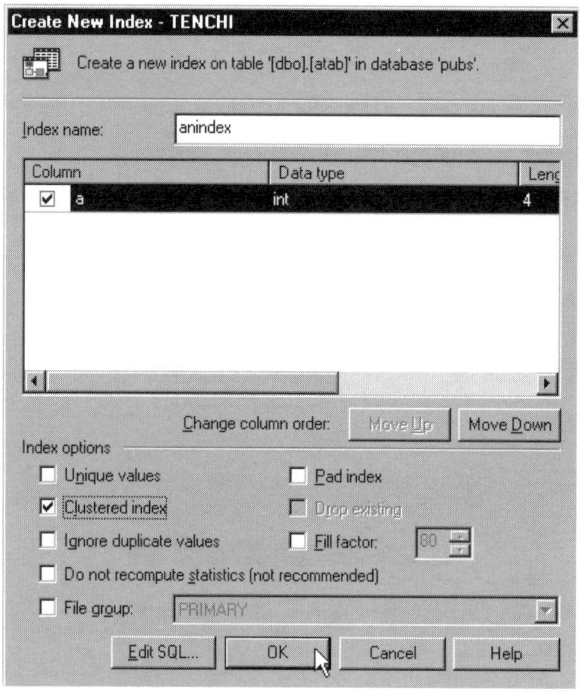

5. Click **OK**.

Index Tuning Wizard

This wizard allows the Enterprise Manager to analyze your databases to determine what indexes the database might benefit from. This is based on allowing SQL Server to analyze the database and the usage of the database. With this information, the Index Tuning Wizard will make recommendations about what indexes will be necessary.

Alerts, Jobs, and Operators

If you would like to get proactive about maintaining your system, you can do so by defining alerts, jobs, and operators.

An *alert* is an event on the SQL Server for which an automated response (job) may be triggered. For example, if the transaction log fills up, you may want to empty it and send an e-mail to yourself so that you are aware that it happened.

A *job* is the task we perform when an alert event occurs. Job steps can be:

- Executable programs
- Operating system (usually Windows NT) commands
- Transact-SQL statements
- Active scripts

An *operator* is an individual responsible for the maintenance the SQL Server(s), and is the person notified when the job runs.

The Enterprise Manager provides a quick and easy interface to define alerts so when a specific error occurs the appropriate operator is notified of the problem. That way many errors can be prevented from escalating into disasters. This same interface will also be able to react to an alert by executing a job. This may often resolve the error before the operator gets the message. For more complete information on alerts, jobs, and operators, see Chapter 13.

Your Maintenance Checklist

This is a recommended task list, and will serve the maintenance purposes of most installations. You should take a look at this list within the scope of your own application(s), and look at the documentation for your own product as well as the business requirements of your organization to decide whether this specific schedule works for you.

One-time only:

- Store your memory configuration parameters someplace permanent.
- Devise and test your disaster recovery scheme.

On-demand:

- Update the table statistics if/when the situation warrants.
- Predefine auto-grow/auto-shrink for your databases.

Daily:

- Check the server activity log.
- Back up your database and transaction logs.
- Get the backups off-site.
- Run preventive maintenance DBCC list. (This is a good thing to run overnight or when a low volume of processing is occurring.)

Weekly:

- Check space utilization of your databases to make sure that the growth you are getting is the growth you expect. Also, verify that the amount of free space is what you expect.
- Store current table information (like the number of rows in each table) so that you can track growth.
- Check/correct table and index fragmentation.

As often as you are able:

- Periodically, shut down and restart the server. It doesn't matter too much if this is daily, weekly, or monthly, but it is important to not only shut down the server, but also to shut down and restart the physical server. This is primarily to clean up memory.

Chapter 3

Configuration Values

Configuration options exist to allow you to tune Microsoft SQL Server 7.0's performance by changing memory or I/O (physical input/output) settings. With release 7.0, more and more experienced production DBAs are simply installing the server and letting it reconfigure itself (Microsoft SQL Server 7.0 is self-tuning). There are a few configuration options that you may want to understand, though, on the chance that you want to second-guess the server. However, it is highly recommended that the default settings be retained, so that the server may tune itself. We categorize the configuration parameters as memory, I/O, or operating system (usually Windows NT) specific.

Memory Configuration Options

The memory manager component of SQL Server allows self-configuration of memory for SQL Server. When SQL Server starts, it determines how much memory it may allocate based on how much memory the operating system and other applications are currently using. Note that this implies that the more you are running on that (presumably NT or Windows 2000) server, the fewer resources are available for Microsoft SQL Server 7.0. As the load on the computer and SQL Server changes, so does the allocated memory.

The following memory configuration options are available for tuning:

Min server memory	This memory option requires the server to start with this minimum amount of memory, as opposed to the default that allows the server to start with all available memory. It can be set to a specific value based on the amount of physical memory and level of activity on your SQL Server. Make sure that this minimum memory is set low enough that it does not suck all available memory from other OS level tasks, as that may also negatively affect Microsoft SQL Server performance. The default setting for min server memory is 0. We recommend the automatic setting, which will always allow NT to operate with as little paging as possible.
Max server memory	This option specifies the maximum amount of memory SQL Server can allocate when it starts and while it runs. It can be set to a specific value if you know there are multiple applications running at the same time as SQL Server and you want to ensure that these applications have sufficient memory to run. If the other applications request memory only as needed, then do not set this server configuration option, because SQL Server will release memory to them as needed. Remember that applications often use whatever memory is available when they start and do not request more if needed. If an application that behaves this way runs on the same computer as Microsoft SQL Server at the same time as SQL Server, set the max server memory server configuration option to a value that guarantees that the memory the application needs is not set aside for SQL Server. The default setting for max server memory is 2147483647. The minimum amount of memory you can specify for max server memory is 4 MB. You must set the max server memory option manually if you are running the full-text search (also called MSSearch) to ensure that the server leaves enough memory for the MSSearch service to run. It must be adjusted in conjunction with the Windows NT virtual memory size to ensure that the virtual memory remaining for full-text search is 1.5 times the physical memory (exclude the virtual memory requirements of the other services on the computer). Try this formula:

Max server memory (cont.)	Total virtual memory—(SQL Server maximum virtual memory + virtual memory requirements of other services) must be greater than or equal to 1.5 times the physical memory.
Max worker threads	Threads are operating system specific processes that enable parallel processing and multi-tasking. This configuration option can be used to specify the number of threads used to support the processes that will be run by users connected to SQL Server. The default setting of 255 can be slightly high for some configurations, depending on the number of concurrent users. Because each worker thread is preallocated, even if it is not being used, memory resources that might be better utilized by other operations, such as the buffer cache, can be unused. Generally, this configuration value should be set to the number of expected concurrent connections. The maximum value for max worker threads is 1024. Finally, note that this parameter has no effect when SQL Server is running on Windows 95/98.
Index create memory	This option controls the amount of memory used by sort operations during index creation. Creating an index on a production system is usually an infrequently performed task, often scheduled as a job to execute during off-peak time. While increasing this number can improve the performance of index creation, if you are not creating indexes, this is a waste of resources. We recommend you keep the min memory per query configuration option at the default, however, so the index creation job will still start even if all the requested memory is not available.
Min memory per query	This configuration option can be used to specify the minimum amount of memory that will be allocated for the execution of any specific query. When many queries are executing concurrently in a system, increasing the value of this parameter can help improve the performance of memory-intensive queries. Do not set the min memory per query server configuration option too high, especially on very busy systems, because the query will have to wait until it can grab the minimum memory requested. If more memory is available than the specified minimum value required to run the query, the query may make use of the additional memory, provided that the additional memory will be used effectively by the query.

You should not set the min server memory and max server memory configuration options to the same value. This would fix the amount of memory allocated to SQL Server. Dynamic memory allocation gives you the best overall performance.

I/O Configuration Options

These server configuration options can be used to tune the operating system's ability to access the disks optimally, thus improving overall server performance.

Max async IO	Synchronous I/O means that you make a request for data, wait for it to be retrieved, then request another one. Asynchronous I/O means that while the server is waiting for one page to be retrieved, it requests other pages, thus doing some work while waiting for pages to come back. This configuration option can be used to configure the maximum number of outstanding asynchronous disk I/O requests that the SQL Server can issue against a file. You should leave this option at the default value of 32. If you have a large number of I/O subsystems with many disks and controllers, the value can be increased to 64 or possibly higher.
Recovery interval	In order to minimize the amount of time it takes the server to come back up after an unexpected or improper shutdown, a process called checkpoint flushes all used data pages from cache (memory) and moves them to disk. The checkpoint is resource intensive, so we control the number of automatic checkpoints with the recovery interval server configuration option. By default, the SQL Server tries to determine the best time to perform a checkpoint. To determine if this is the appropriate setting, you can monitor disk write activity on your database files by using Windows NT Performance Monitor. If any disk utilization reaches 100 percent, you can assume your performance is not optimal. Increasing this parameter (the number of minutes between checkpoints) can improve overall performance in this situation. You should continue to monitor performance after making this modification to determine if the new value has had a positive effect on performance.

Configuring Server Performance Using Windows NT Options

You can set Windows NT options on the server to maximize throughput or to configure server tasking.

Maximize Throughput

When you install Microsoft SQL Server 7.0, SQL Server setup automatically configures Microsoft Windows NT to maximize throughput for network applications. (Note that the network is a very likely bottleneck in a high-volume environment.) This helps the server accommodate more connections. Maximizing throughput for network applications is recommended for Microsoft SQL Server, but you can change this setting if you know enough about your NT server. As this is not recommended, it is beyond the scope for this book.

Note that if your application makes use of the full-text search feature (this is an enhanced ability to search for character strings quickly in a database), the Windows NT Server configuration must be set for maximizing throughput for network applications and must not be changed.

Note: The Windows NT Server configuration setting does not apply to computers running Windows NT Workstation. For more information, see your Windows NT documentation.

Configure Server Tasking

If you plan to connect to SQL Server from a local client (the same computer as the server), you can improve processing time by setting up the server to run foreground and background applications with equal priority. SQL Server, which runs as a background application, then runs at equal priority to other applications running in the foreground.

Note: If your application uses an ODBC client connection to the same system that the server is on, set the ODBC Server name to (local), which does not use the network layer and will save a little time.

This means that no program will become starved for resources at the expense of another, which is a good reason for running Microsoft SQL Server 7.0 on its own physical server. Note that when you run SQL Server setup, server tasking is set to none (the SQL Server default), which gives foreground and background programs equal processor time. You can set the server tasking setting to maximum (the Microsoft Windows NT default), which gives foreground applications the most processor time, but this is not recommended. (Again, this is an NT-tunable task, is not recommended, and is beyond the scope of this book.)

Configure Virtual Memory

Windows NT virtual memory size should be configured based on the programs (services) concurrently running on the specific computer. Microsoft documentation on this is mixed; in one place, it recommends that you set virtual memory on the server to 1.5 times the amount of physical memory installed in the computer. In another, it suggests that this value be set to the amount of physical memory plus 12 MB. This author recommends that you set this to a flat 512 MB. Above this number, it takes more time for the system to manage the paging file than it helps, and we have even seen it cause problems. So, if your system has more than 512 MB of RAM, set your paging file to 512 and be done with it.

Additionally, if you are using the full-text search feature and will be running the Microsoft Search Service so that you can do full-text indexing and querying, consider configuring the virtual memory size to 3 times the amount of physical memory installed in the computer, and the SQL Server max server memory server configuration option to 1.5 times the physical memory (half the virtual memory size setting).

If you get the following Windows NT error, it means that virtual memory is configured too low:

```
Your system is running low on virtual memory. Please close some
applications. You can then start the System option in the Control Panel
and choose the Virtual Memory button to create an additional paging
file or increase the size of your current paging file.
```

Note that this can also be caused by using a program that was written for a 16-bit operating system (that is, an older application), which is still limited to the high memory location between 640 KB and 1 MB. Nothing can be done about this. Also, there is a desktop pool registry entry that needs to be increased from 256 KB to 1 MB.

The memory configuration parameters can be modified by clicking on the appropriate server in the Enterprise Manager, then clicking on Tools in the menu bar and selecting SQL Server Configuration Properties.

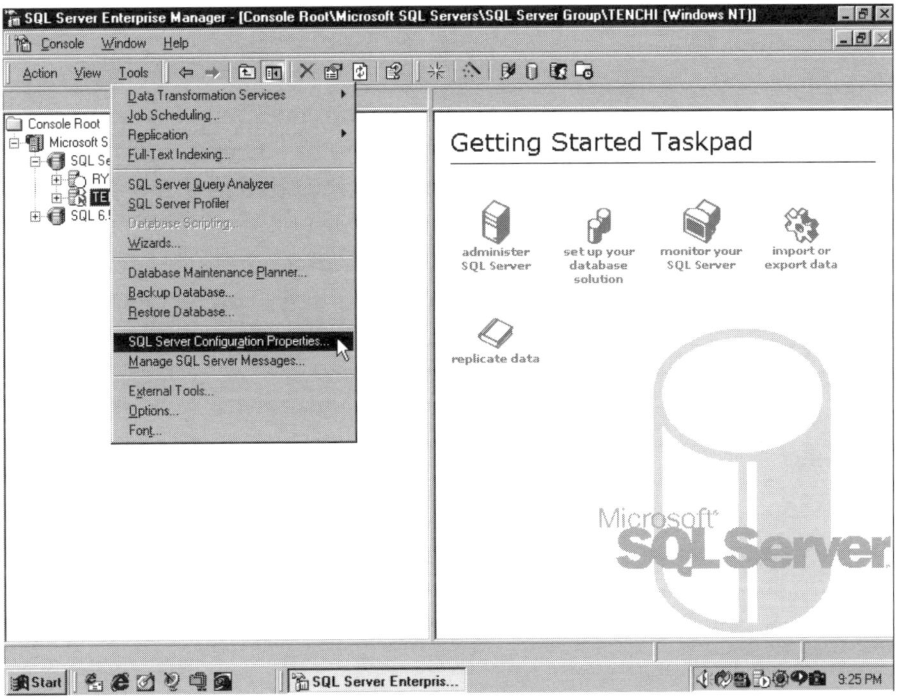

Then click the Memory tab to display the memory configuration options.

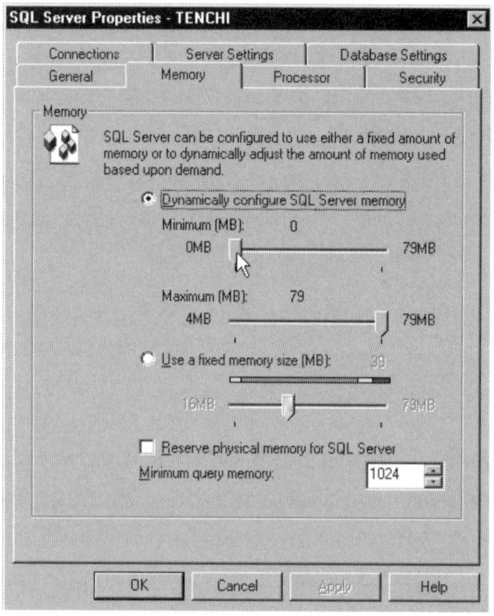

The maximum and minimum memory configuration options can be altered by dragging the appropriate bar. However, since memory is an autoconfiguring option, it is recommended that the defaults be kept. This means that SQL Server will dynamically configure memory. Remember, in the long run, we recommend that you do not change any of these options unless you are specifically required to by your application vendor.

Chapter 4

Activity Monitoring

Once a SQL Server is up and running, it is necessary to make sure that it is running well. The server should be operating at its best. While the SQL Server is pretty good at making sure it runs as efficiently as possible, there is one key factor that the SQL Server has minimal control over: how the users work with the databases. Since each user that connects to the server will require resources of some kind, it is necessary to keep an eye on how much the server is being used and when. Sometimes, these kinds of checks will illustrate that a server is running well and doesn't require much change. Other times, the server may be reaching the limits of its physical capabilities. In this case, an upgrade may be required for the server.

Monitoring Tools

SQL Server provides tools for monitoring the activity on the server. They include the SQL Enterprise Manager and NT Performance Monitor.

SQL Enterprise Manager

The SQL Enterprise Manager provides a quick and easy way to monitor the usage of the database server. It allows for the checking of the current activity of the system. Over time, this will allow an administrator to determine what is normal and what is abnormal usage of the server at any given time. For instance, an administrator may be aware that there are 100 people that access the server and during the late afternoon up to half of them may be connected to the server at once. This implies that having around 50 people connected to the server is a normal occurrence. However, if 200 connections were simultaneously made to the server, maybe suspicion is warranted.

Aside from just determining how many connections have been made to the SQL Server, information can also be obtained about what tasks those connections are performing. This can include what type of command was run, when the connection logged in, and when they executed their last commands. Also vital is the determination of whether a connection is blocking the work of another connection.

To check for existing processes on the SQL Server:

1. In Enterprise Manager, expand the **Management** folder.
2. Expand the **Current Activity** folder.
3. Select **Process Info**.

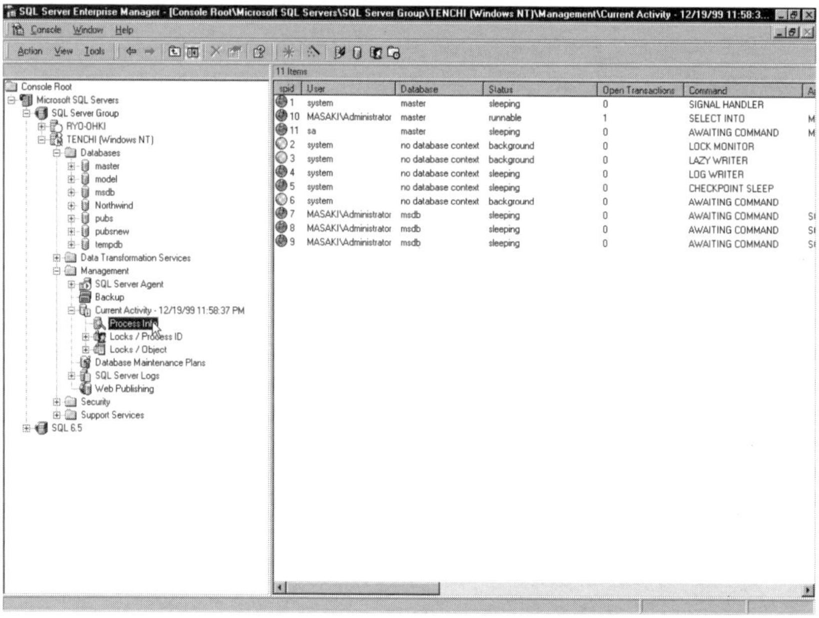

Note that each connection has a *spid*. The spid that you see here is the system process ID. This system process ID distinguishes one connection as being different from another. The Blocked By column determines the connection that is preventing a task from completing. The Blocking column indicates the process being blocked by the current one.

Each one of the processes can also hold locks. When information is being read or written, a lock is held on the data. Depending on the kind of lock, this may allow only one user to be able to work with a specific piece of information. Or it may allow everyone to be able to read the same piece of information. Often locks are used to prevent two or more people from changing the exact same piece of information at the exact same time. Locks can also have different sizes. Some can be as large as a database, while others may only be as large as a single row of information. The type of lock is determined by the type of command executed. The size of the lock is determined by the SQL Server.

Locks can be viewed by expanding the Locks/Process ID folder or the Locks/Object folder under Current Activity. A list of the different locks owned by a particular process is provided:

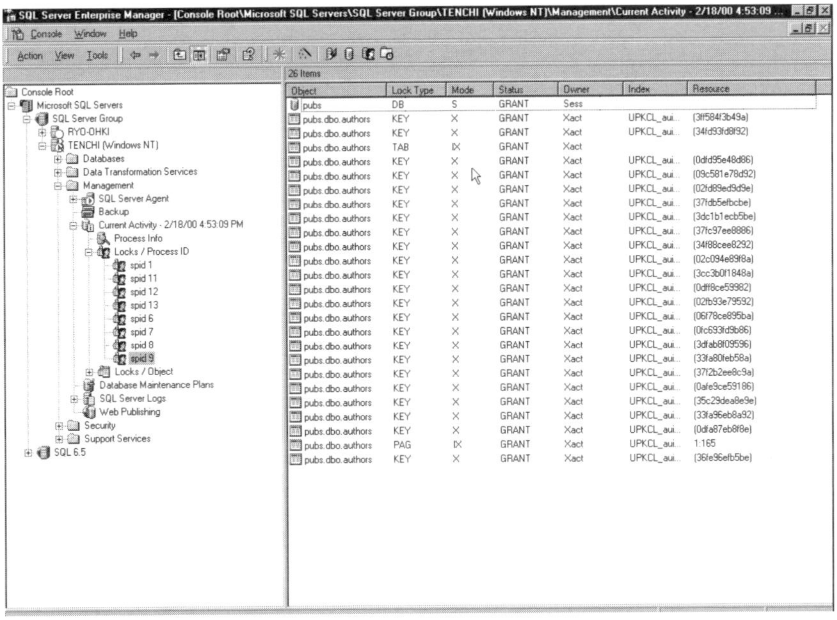

or a list of locks presently held on a particular object:

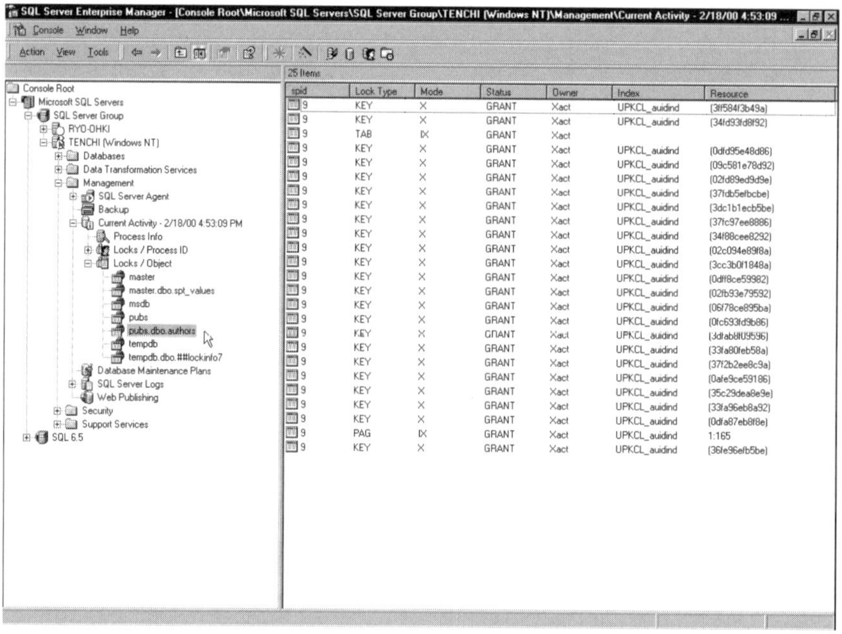

Sometimes if a process is blocking another, the system may seem to pause. This is normal. Often SQL Server will not allow newer users to work with data until the present user is done working with it. However, if the task is critical or if the original task is not running correctly, tasks can be killed to make way for other tasks.

To find blocking processes:

1. Expand the **Management** folder.
2. Expand the **Current Activity** folder.
3. Expand the **Locks/Process ID** folder.

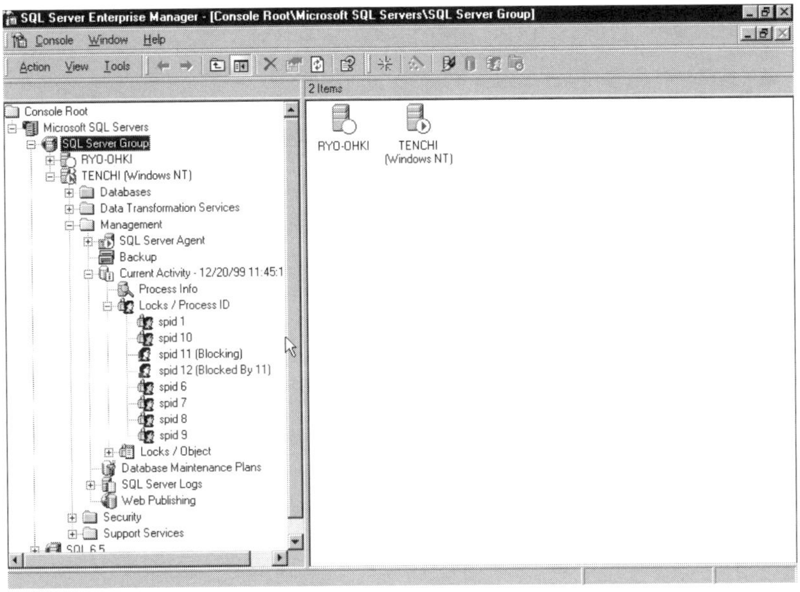

Note that spid 11 is labeled as Blocking and spid 12 is the process waiting for 11 to complete.

To eliminate blocking processes:

1. Select **Process Info**.
2. Select the blocking process (in this case spid 11).

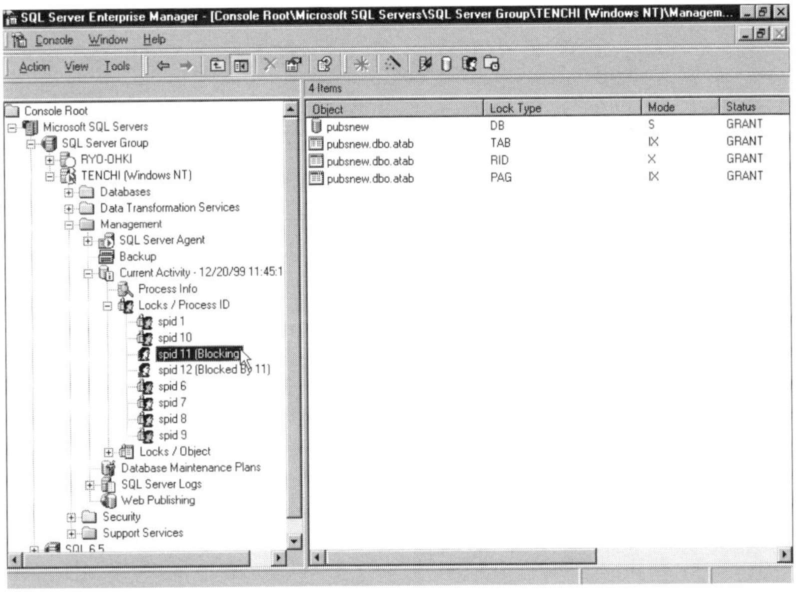

3. Click **Action** on the menu bar.
4. Select **Kill Process**.

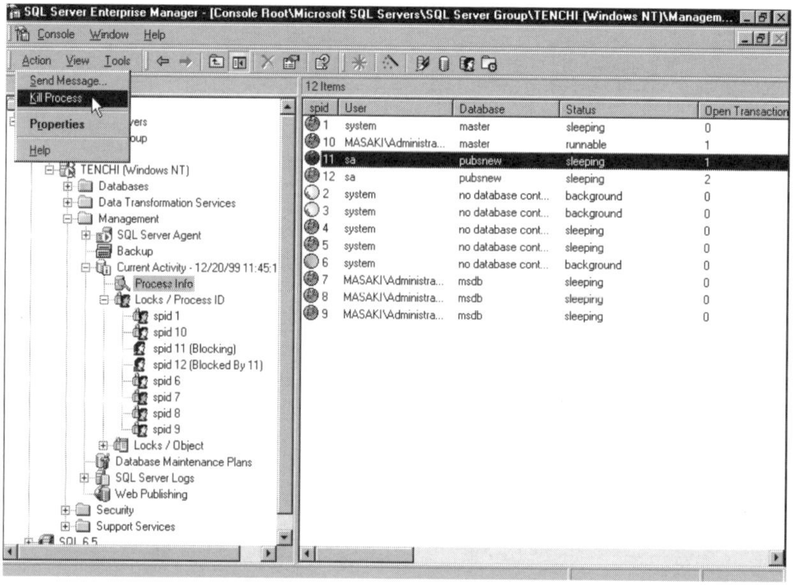

5. Click **Yes** to eliminate the process.

Note: Killing processes is a very dangerous business. The changes made by the removed processes can be lost. Sometimes the processes cannot be killed without shutting down and restarting the server. Do this only when absolutely necessary.

NT Performance Monitor

Another way to monitor performance of the SQL Server is to monitor its performance on the NT Performance Monitor (NT systems only). The NT Performance Monitor is a tool provided by Windows NT and has connections to the SQL Server to monitor its performance. It produces a constant line graph that measures rises and drops in the server's activity.

To access the NT Performance Monitor:

1. Click the **Start** button.
2. Select **Programs**.
3. Select **MS SQL Server 7.0**.
4. Select **Performance Monitor**.

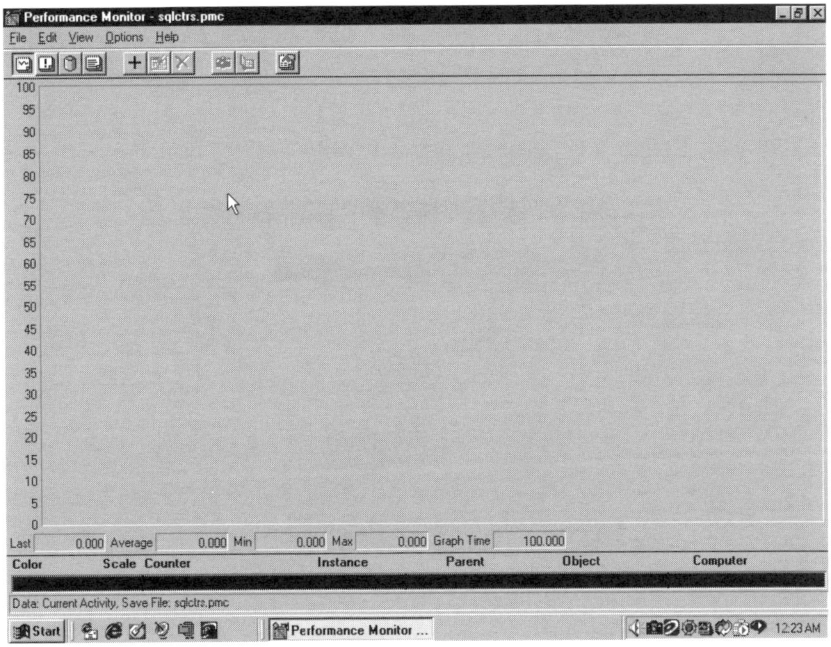

To add a counter:

1. Click the plus sign (+) on the toolbar.

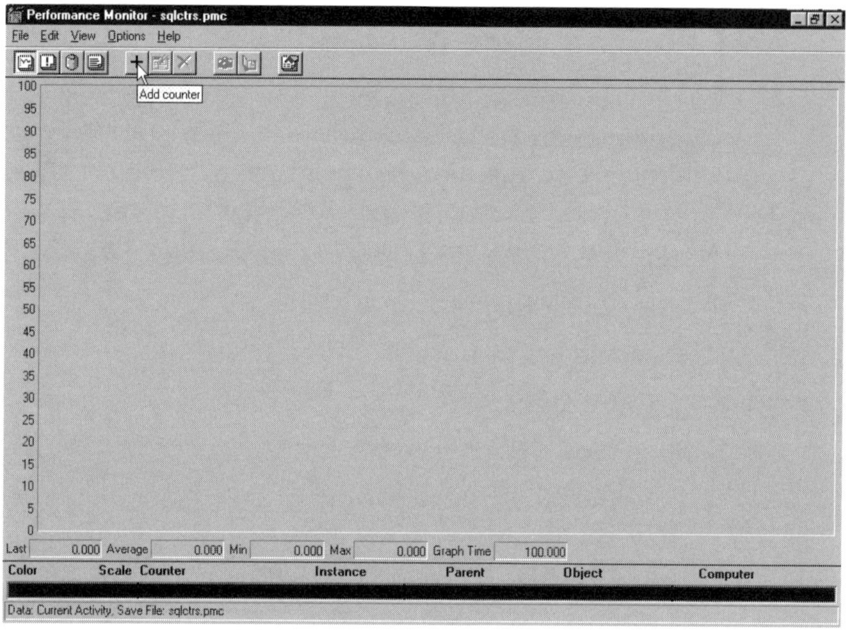

2. Select a type of object from the Object box.

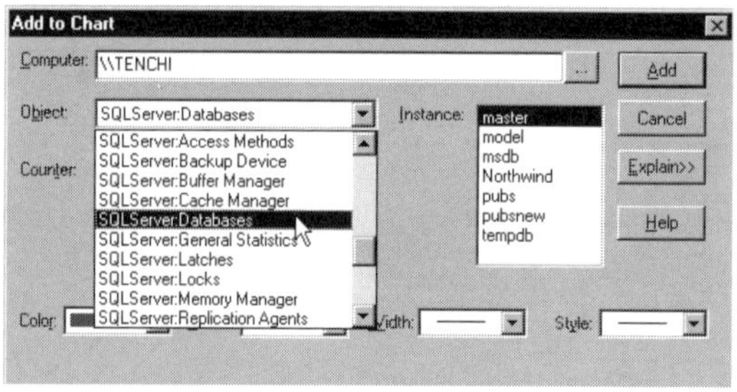

3. Select a counter from the Counter box.
4. Select a particular database for the counter to track.

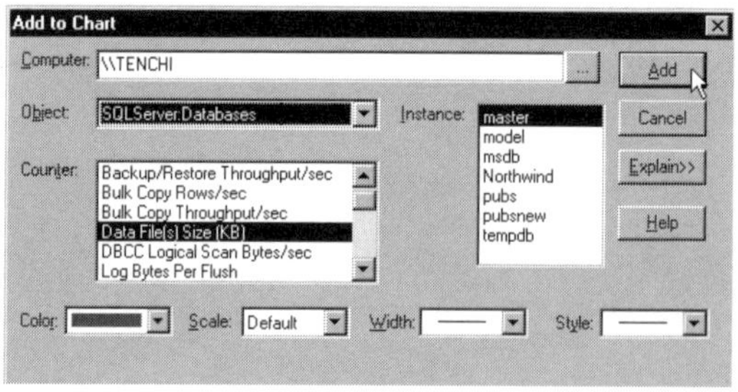

5. Click **Add** to add the graph.
6. Click **Done** when finished.

This graph will now display the percentage of the log that is full for the database. As the percentage increases, so will the height of the line in the graph.

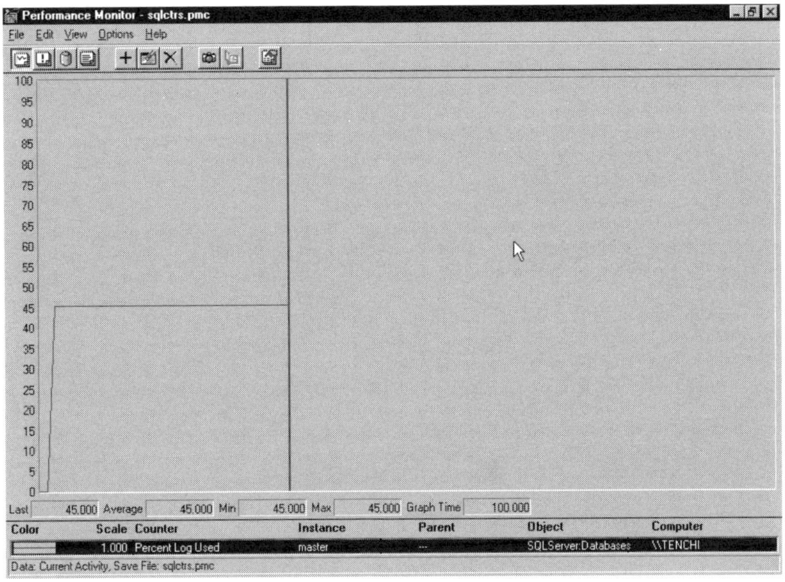

Note that this tool is an NT-based tool so it is not used exclusively for SQL Server. There are counters available for the NT system as well as any other programs that may be installed.

In order to make sure the server is performing at its best, it is a good idea to watch and see how the server performs at different times during the day. This also includes watching the usage of the server. Keeping track of how many users, what they are doing, and when they are doing it will help determine the normal performance level for your server. This will help identify when the usage is out of the norm as well as how resources are being used. Keeping track of these measurements will help determine when the server needs to be changed to meet changing needs.

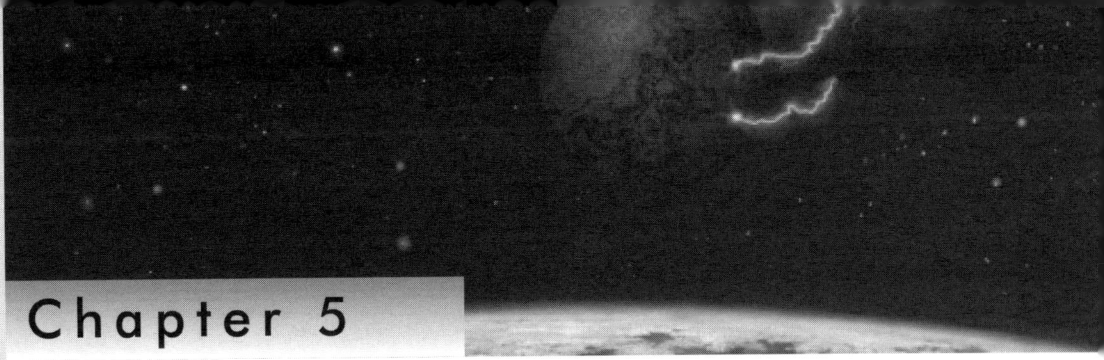

Chapter 5

Monitoring Your Error Log

Each time you start SQL Server it creates a record of all server-level information. This is called the error log. You need to become familiar with this log as it contains vital information that will tell you how SQL Server is running. This error log tells you whether vital processes have been completed successfully. Some of these operations include backups, restore operations, batch commands, scripts, and other processes.

Accessing the Error Log

You can open the error log through any script editor or through SQL Server Enterprise Manager. This is the easiest route for you to view your error log. You open the log by performing the following steps:

1. Click the **Start** button and select **Programs|Microsoft SQL Server 7.0|Enterprise Manager.**

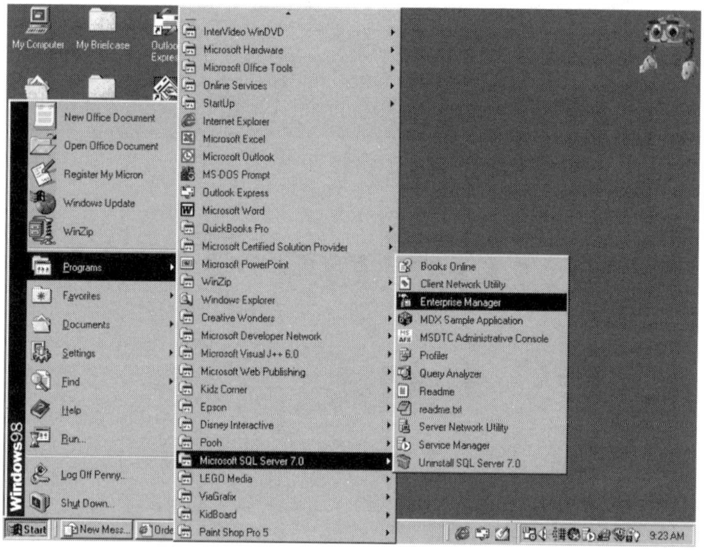

2. Select **Microsoft SQL Servers|SQL Server Group|SQLServerName**, then click on **SQL Server Logs**.

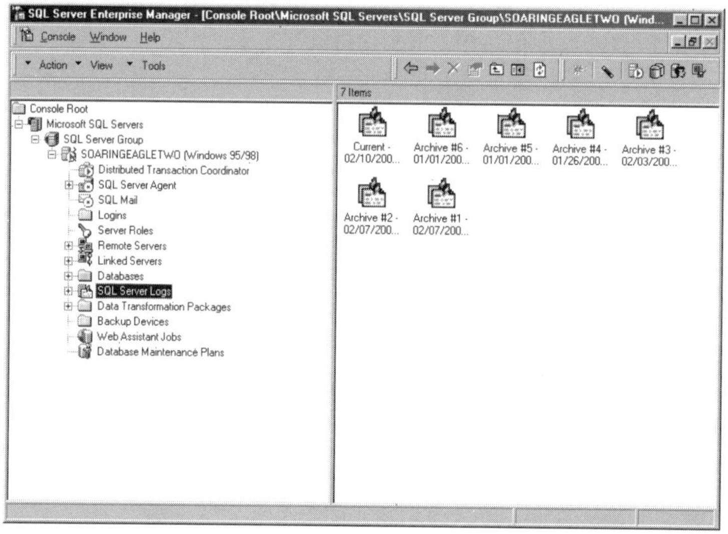

You will see icons to the right of the directory. The current log is the one that is running right now. The current log is started as soon as SQL Server is started. Each time SQL Server is stopped, the log is saved and becomes an archived log. SQL Server keeps six archived logs for you. It gives the most recent archived log a number 1 extension and the next archived log a number 2 extension. This continues with the succeeding logs. The current log has no numbered extension.

Click on the Current icon and look at the log. Try to familiarize yourself with the appearance and the language structure. (Please note this is a resizable window and you may have to stretch the window in order to read all of the information).

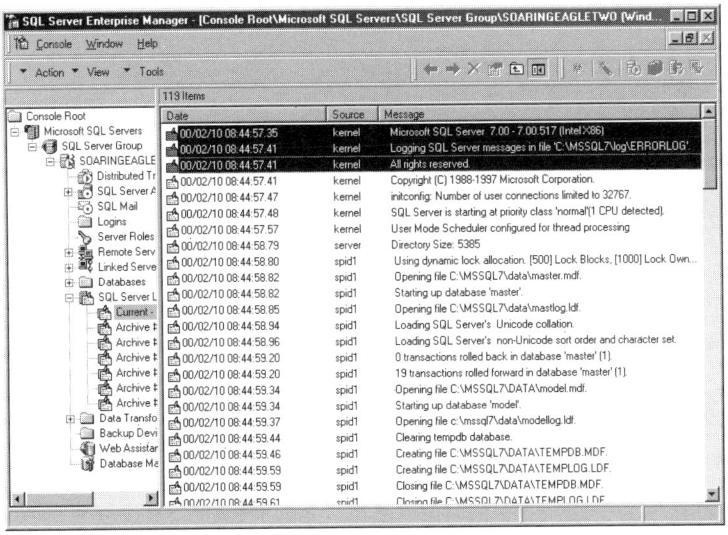

Error Log Messages

The following are a few samples of items found in the error log that you should get used to reading and understanding what they mean to your system's running condition.

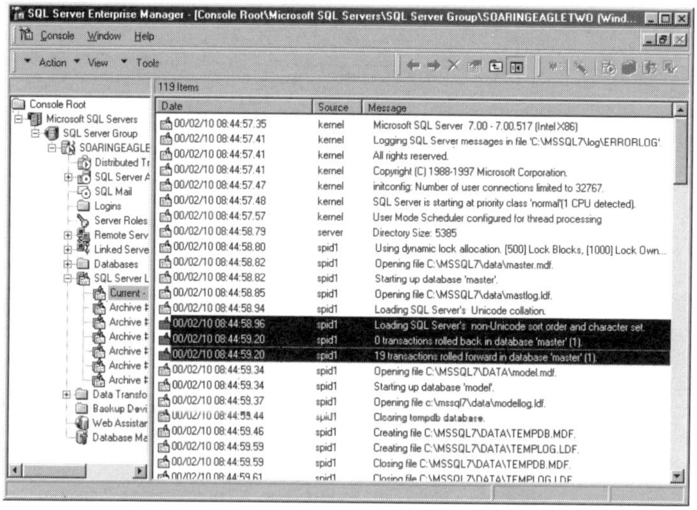

When the server starts, it takes time to synchronize the transaction log with the data. This sounds complex, but it just means that the server makes sure that any completed transaction in memory at the time the server went down is applied to the data on disk. This process is called recovery and is an automatic process that occurs on every database whenever the server is restarted.

There are some warnings that are necessary to see, but not to panic over. The Warning: override autoexec procedures skipped is an example of one of them. This warning just states that an autoexec procedure was skipped (see below) and has no major implications for the running of this SQL Server.

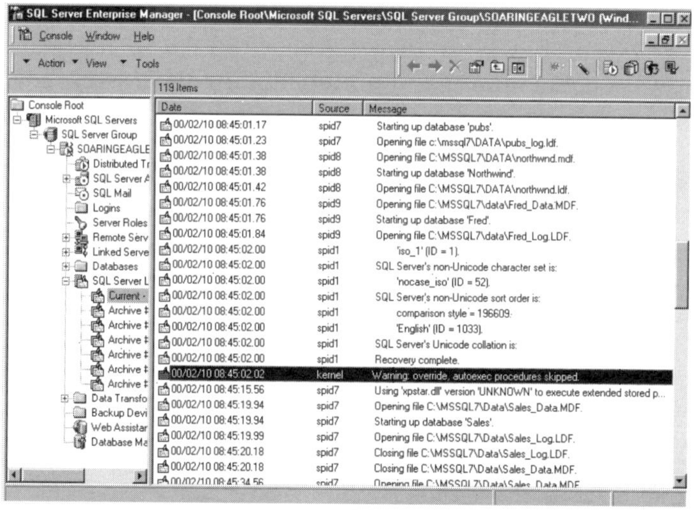

The Recovery complete message is an important message to look for. It means that the SQL Server was started and all startup procedures have been completed. This message gives you a level of comfort knowing that at this point in time your database system is running.

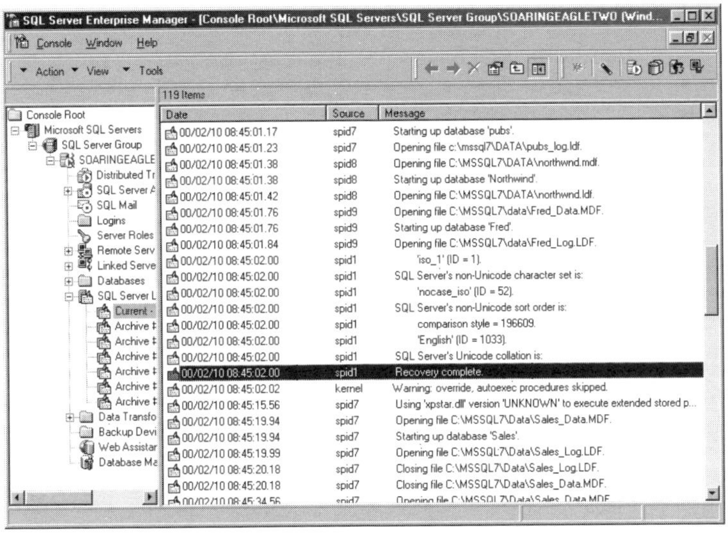

Severity Level Error Messages

Severity level error messages provide a way of informing you as to the type and seriousness of the problem that your SQL Server has encountered. The following table lists the type and reason for each severity level.

Severity Levels	Type	Explanation
0	Not visible on SQL Server 7.0	
1-10	Information	Caused by mistakes in the information that you have entered.
11- 16	User generated errors	These messages can be caused and corrected by the user (anyone connected to the SQL Server at the time the message is sent, not limited to and including a data entry user).

Severity Levels	Type	Explanation
17	Resource Error	SQL Server has run out of resources, disk space for the database, or locks, or has exceeded the limits set by the system administrator.
18	Nonfatal Internal Error Detected	Internal software problem.
19	SQL Server Error in Resource	This means that an internal limit has been exceeded and must be corrected by your system administrator or your system support provider.
20-25	System Problems; Fatal Errors	The processes (the set of programs that were written to complete a task) have failed. The program(s) are paused and a record of the error is kept, and then the program is terminated; SQL Server closes and may not reconnect (depending on the seriousness of the problem).
20	Fatal Error in Current Process	The problem has only affected the current process.
21	Fatal Error in Database (dbid) Process	A problem has affected all processes in the current database. This does not mean that the whole database has been corrupted.
22	Fatal Error Table Integrity Suspect	This message signifies that the table or index specified has been damaged by either a software or hardware problem. Run DBCC CHECKDB to discover if other objects in the database are also damaged. If the problem is in cache only and not on the disk, then restarting SQL Server will correct the problem. You may have to restore the database. If restarting does not help, you may be able to solve the problem by destroying the object that is specified in the error message.
23	Fatal Error Database Integrity Suspect	The entire database is suspect due to damage caused by a hardware or software problem.

Severity Levels	Type	Explanation
24	Fatal Hardware Error	Media failure. The database may have to be reloaded. Call your hardware vendor for support!

This may be a good time to remind you that backing up your database and getting a copy off-site is vital. As you can see from just these few samples of what can go wrong, it is imperative to develop and maintain a database backup system.

Accessing the Application Log

Although the SQL Server error log contains more complete information about the events of the processes occurring in SQL Server, you may also find the application log output essential in tracking down the root of the problems that are occurring on the Windows NT system.

To read the NT Event Viewer application log:

1. Click the **Start** button.
2. Select **Programs|Administrative Tools (Common)|Event Viewer**.

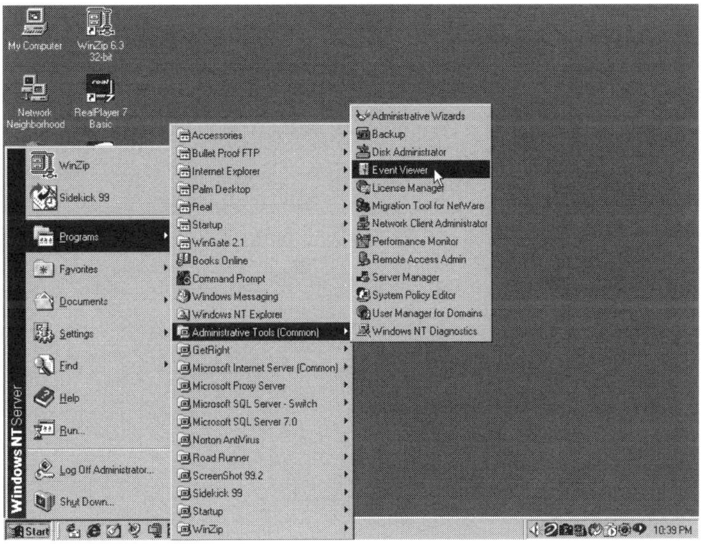

The Event Viewer allows you to filter the information that is shown in the application log. You can use filters for event types such as warnings, information, errors, success audits, and failure audits. Since both logs are time stamped for all recorded events you can match process times and date messages to discover the root of your problems. Many of the common errors you will need to deal with are detailed in Appendix A.

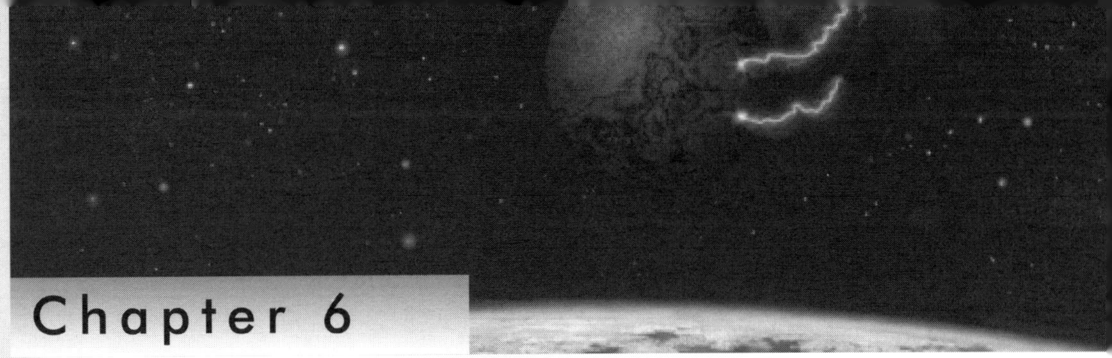

Chapter 6

Disaster Recovery Plan

If you are really lucky, you will never have to open up your disaster recovery plan after you've thought it through and written it. In fact, this is a part of the job that you hope is a waste of your time. As a point of reference, here is Garbus' law of disaster preparedness:

"The less you prepare for a disaster, the more likely it is to happen. Curiously, however, the more you prepare for a disaster, the more likely it is to happen."

Better to be prepared, don't you think? It's a good idea to have a written disaster recovery plan so that if there is trouble, panic does not need to set in; you can simply open the plan, and follow it.

If your transaction volume is low and you have the ability to duplicate a day's transactions easily, you may never need more disaster recovery than to reload the database. However, this is a decision to make after you take into account all types of disasters you might have to deal with and accept the risks accordingly.

What Can Go Wrong?

There are actually a limited number of things you can do if there is a disaster. What you need to do is to make a plan that categorizes the types of disasters and the appropriate responses to those disasters. First, for convenience, here is a relatively complete list of potential disasters (talk to the practical joker in your office for others):

Loss of Hardware

The physical machine is:

- Stolen
- Dysfunctional (chip/board failure)
- Has a disk failure

Note: Disk failure can be mitigated by utilizing disk mirroring, which is highly recommended. Disk mirroring is performed at the NT level, by telling the NT operating system that you want a pair of disks tied together at the operating system level and used for *fail-over*. This means that if one disk fails, you want the other one to take over for it immediately.

- Burned in a fire
- Drowned in a flood (or by a sprinkler system, activated environmentally or otherwise)
- Shaken (not stirred) by an earthquake

If you lose your hardware, it is decision time, and you should be ready in advance to make this call. Do you try to fix the hardware or do you go with new hardware? Based on your agreement with your hardware vendor, decide when you try to fix versus replace, based on how long it will take to replace the hardware and how long you can wait for it to be repaired. Plan ahead for how you will act in specific situations.

Loss of SQL Server

- The operating system *blue screens*. This means that the operating system had an unrecoverable error, which led to a blue screen describing the problem, which forces you to restart NT.

Note: Observation has shown a very high percentage (upwards of 90%) of NT blue screens seem to be caused by a faulty piece of equipment, one that's not on NT's compatibility list, or a faulty driver for a piece of hardware.

- The Microsoft SQL Server crashes. Sometimes an error is severe enough to cause a server to simply shut itself down or system files or tables become corrupt.

Every once in a while, the server will crash. This may never happen to you, but in a high-volume environment, I know places that never have this problem and others that need to restart their operating systems a few times per week.

If the server shuts itself down, simply restart it, whether it is at the NT level or the SQL Server level. After the server restarts (it will restart after NT restarts if you restart NT) you should look at the error log and verify that all databases started normally. Note that a sudden shutdown of the server can cause damage to the databases, and you should verify that it has not.

Loss of Power

- Somebody forgets to pay the bill
- There is a problem at the power plant
- Lightning strikes the power line
- A squirrel chews through a transformer

In case of loss of power, hopefully you have been notified by the sharp beeping of your UPS, and have shut down first the SQL Server, then the NT box. A UPS (uninterruptible power supply) is essential; in case of a loss of power, you do not want your server to suddenly shut down. This can cause data loss or database corruption. You can get a UPS from any computer supply shop or, these days, office supply store. If you spend a bit more on your UPS, you can get one that automatically shuts down the box when there is a power failure. Then, when the power comes back on, simply turn the box back on.

Loss of Data

- Database corruption
- A user deletes something that shouldn't have been deleted
- Sabotage

Let's Fix the Problem!

Now, here is your list of remedies, in decreasing order of effort and aggravation:

- Build a new physical server

This means you buy new hardware, because you've given up on the old box.

- Build a new database server

This means that you need to reinstall Microsoft SQL Server, as you did the first time. This is typically the result of losing the physical disks upon which the server is installed.

- Restore the database

Refer to Chapter 8 for the restore technique.

- Run DBCC with the fix option

Refer to Chapter 2 for specifics on how to run DBCC with the fix option.

Of all the above options, it is most likely that you will have to restore the database.

Disaster/Remedy Grid

What we have, then, is a list of potential problems along with the list of potential solutions. Remember to try the least-invasive solution first. You may want to start with the following chart and modify it to suit your own needs.

	Rebuild Physical Server	Rebuild SQL Server	Restore Database	Run DBCC with "Fix" Option
Loss of Hardware				
Disk			(After replacing the damaged disk)	
Anything other than disk	●	●	●	

	Rebuild Physical Server	Rebuild SQL Server	Restore Database	Run DBCC with "Fix" Option
Loss of SQL Server (If the Server error log reports an error)			2nd (if DBCC fails)	1st
Loss of Power			2nd (if DBCC fails)	1st
The server shuts down suddenly			2nd (if DBCC fails)	1st
Loss of Data			●	
Preventive DBCC shows an error			2nd (if DBCC fails)	1st

Recommended Approach

More generally, here are the four basic types of problems and instructions for how you should proceed if they are encountered. You should look at this list when everything is functioning normally and decide whether these solutions will be the best for your site or if you need to rewrite them to suit your specific needs.

Damage to hardware	Diagnose, contacting your hardware vendor if possible, and then replace the damaged part.
Hardware catastrophe	Replace hardware, reload all necessary software, and restore from backup (very important to ensure backup media are compatible between old and new system).
Data corruption	Your only option here is to determine the last known point in time you were able to trust your data, and then restore from tape.
Software catastrophe	Reinstall the server; restore the database from tape. Discuss expectations with management prior to this occurrence.

Though there are ways to repair your system after disaster strikes, the best disaster recovery plan is to avoid disaster as much as possible by following your preventive maintenance regimen.

Chapter 7

The Database Consistency Checker (DBCC)

The Database Consistency Checker (DBCC) is a tool that verifies the internal consistency of your database. This is probably the single most technical part of the book, because this is where we talk about the specific tasks that check the physical storage structures. Like disaster recovery, you hope that the DBCC never catches a problem, but on the off chance that it does, you want to repair the problem sooner rather than later. Problems caught early can often be fixed; problems caught late often snowball into complete disasters. Chapter 2 showed you how to run DBCCs quickly and easily, so here we talk about the options, what you are doing, and why.

DBCC Commands

For each database, you have to run the following:

DBCC CHECKALLOC	The data on the SQL Server are broken up into units called pages, which are 8,196 bytes in size (think of a byte as one character of information, like the period at the end of this sentence). Each page is a part of the database, but is also part of a data structure like a table or index. This DBCC task checks the allocation pages (which helps the server determine which pages are free), as well as the usage of each individual page in each database.This does not need to be run if you run DBCC CHECKDB, as it is now a subset of that command.
DBCC CHECKCATALOG	Information about how the data is stored is contained inside the database in special tables called system tables. This DBCC function checks for consistency in and between the system tables in each database.Run this for every database, not just your production database. It catches a wide variety of possible errors and repairs them. In fact, go ahead and run it with the repair option; it should not hurt anything, and will fix the database automatically.
DBCC CHECKDB	This option checks the allocation (see DBCC CHECKALLOC) and structural integrity of all the objects (tables and indexes) in the specified database. Run this for every database, not just your production database.
DBCC CHECKFILEGROUP	Sometimes databases are divided up into filegroups for the purpose of controlling data placement or growth. This option is a subset of DBCC CHECKDB, which checks the allocation and structural integrity of all tables in the specified filegroup in the current database. If you run DBCC CHECKDB, you do not need to run this.

DBCC CHECKALLOC

Syntax

```
DBCC CHECKALLOC
( 'database_name'
[, NOINDEX
|
{ REPAIR_ALLOW_DATA_LOSS
```

```
| REPAIR_FAST
| REPAIR_REBUILD
}]
) [WITH {ALL_ERRORMSGS | NO_INFOMSGS}]
```

Arguments

'database_name'
: The name of the database you want to check. Defaults to the current database. You should specify this to be sure you're checking the right database.

NOINDEX
: This option is ignored, so don't use it.

REPAIR_ALLOW_DATA_LOSS | REPAIR_FAST | REPAIR_REBUILD
: Instructs the server to repair the errors it finds. You should use the REPAIR_REBUILD option as it is the most complete option.

WITH ALL_ERRORMSGS | NO_INFOMSGS
: Specifies an option for error messages. ALL_ERRORMESSAGES shows all error messages (if you don't specify this, SQL Server displays a maximum of 200 error messages per object, which is recommended). NO_INFOMSGS hides all output.

If you do not suppress output, your output will look something like this. Note that you do not need to do anything unless the output reports errors.

```
DBCC checkalloc (pubs2)
DBCC results for 'pubs2'.
***************************************************************
Table sysobjects Object ID 1.
Index ID 1 FirstIAM (1:4) Root (1:6) Dpages 2 Sort 0.
Data level 1. 4 data pages in 0 extents.
Index ID 2 FirstIAM (1:15) Root (1:14) Dpages 1 Sort 0.
Index ID 2. 2 index pages in 0 extents.
Index ID 3 FirstIAM (1:34) Root (1:33) Dpages 1 Sort 0.
Index ID 3. 2 index pages in 0 extents.
Total number of extents is 0.
***************************************************************
```

```
Table sysindexes Object ID 2.
Index ID 1 FirstIAM (1:12) Root (1:13) Dpages 2 Sort 0.
Data level 1. 4 data pages in 0 extents.
Index ID 255 FirstIAM (1:28) Root (1:16) Dpages 0 Sort 0.
Index ID 255. 4 index pages in 1 extents.
Total number of extents is 1.
***************************************************************
Table syscolumns Object ID 3.
Index ID 1 FirstIAM (1:26) Root (1:27) Dpages 8 Sort 0.
Data level 1. 10 data pages in 1 extents.
Index ID 2 FirstIAM (1:36) Root (1:35) Dpages 6 Sort 0.
Index ID 2. 8 index pages in 0 extents.
Total number of extents is 1.
***************************************************************
Table systypes Object ID 4.
Index ID 1 FirstIAM (1:30) Root (1:31) Dpages 1 Sort 0.
Data level 1. 3 data pages in 0 extents.
Index ID 2 FirstIAM (1:38) Root (1:37) Dpages 1 Sort 0.
Index ID 2. 2 index pages in 0 extents.
Total number of extents is 0.
```

DBCC CHECKCATALOG

Syntax

```
DBCC CHECKCATALOG
( 'database_name'
) [WITH NO_INFOMSGS]
```

Arguments

'database_name'
: The name of the database you want to check. Defaults to the current database. You should specify this to be sure you're checking the right database.

WITH NO_INFOMSGS
: Hides all the output.

If you do not suppress output, your output will look something like this. Note that you do not need to do anything unless the output reports errors. Also note there is not much output from CHECKCATALOG.

```
DBCC checkcatalog (pubs2)
DBCC results for 'pubs2'.
DBCC execution completed. If DBCC printed error messages, contact your
system administrator.
```

DBCC CHECKDB

Syntax

```
DBCC CHECKDB
( 'database_name'
[, NOINDEX
| { REPAIR_ALLOW_DATA_LOSS
| REPAIR_FAST
| REPAIR_REBUILD
}]
) [WITH {ALL_ERRORMSGS | NO_INFOMSGS}]
```

Arguments

'database_name'

The name of the database you want to check. Defaults to the current database. You should specify this to be sure you're checking the right database.

NOINDEX

Specifies that non-clustered indexes for non-system tables should not be checked.

Don't do this. It's for folks with databases so big they do not have the time to run a full CHECKDB every night).

REPAIR_ALLOW_DATA_LOSS | REPAIR_FAST| REPAIR_REBUILD

Instructs the server to repair the errors it finds. You should use the REPAIR_REBUILD option as it is the most complete option.

WITH ALL_ERRORMSGS | NO_INFOMSGS

Specifies an option for error messages. ALL_ERRORMESSAGES shows all error messages (if you don't specify this, SQL Server displays a maximum of 200 error messages per object, which is recommended). NO_INFOMSGS hides all output.

If you do not suppress output, your output will look something like this. Note that you do not need to do anything unless the output reports errors.

```
DBCC checkdb (pubs2)
DBCC results for 'pubs2'.
DBCC results for 'sysobjects'.
There are 112 rows in 2 pages for object 'sysobjects'.
DBCC results for 'sysindexes'.
There are 52 rows in 2 pages for object 'sysindexes'.
DBCC results for 'syscolumns'.
There are 538 rows in 8 pages for object 'syscolumns'.
DBCC results for 'systypes'.
There are 27 rows in 1 pages for object 'systypes'.
DBCC results for 'syscomments'.
There are 150 rows in 18 pages for object 'syscomments'.
DBCC results for 'sysfiles1'.
There are 3 rows in 1 pages for object 'sysfiles1'.
DBCC results for 'syspermissions'.
There are 74 rows in 1 pages for object 'syspermissions'.
DBCC results for 'sysusers'.
```

You will occasionally see messages here that indicate system tables being corrected, or problems caused by people accessing the database while the command is being run. In general, you do not need to take action unless the severity is over 19, and at that point you should check your systems administration guide for instructions as to how to proceed.

DBCC CHECKFILEGROUP

Syntax

```
DBCC CHECKFILEGROUP
( [{'filegroup' | filegroup_id}] [, NOINDEX]
) [WITH {ALL_ERRORMSGS | NO_INFOMSGS}]
```

Arguments

'filegroup'
: The name of the filegroup you want to check. Note that filegroups are database-specific.

filegroup_id
: This is the filegroup identification number (ID) for the filegroup we are going to check. You can obtain filegroup_id from either the Filegroup_Id function or the sysfilegroups system table in the database containing the filegroup.

NOINDEX
: Specifies that non-clustered indexes for non-system tables should not be checked.

  Don't do this. It is for folks with databases so big they do not have the time to run a full CHECKDB every night.

WITH ALL_ERRORMSGS | NO_INFOMSGS
: Specifies an option for error messages. ALL_ERRORMESSAGES shows all error messages (if you don't specify this, SQL Server displays a maximum of 200 error messages per object, which is recommended). NO_INFOMSGS hides all output.

If you do not suppress output, your output will look something like this. Note that you do not need to do anything unless the output reports errors.

```
DBCC checkfilegroup ('PRIMARY')
DBCC results for 'master'.
DBCC results for 'sysobjects'.
There are 923 rows in 14 pages for object 'sysobjects'.
DBCC results for 'sysindexes'.
```

```
There are 85 rows in 3 pages for object 'sysindexes'.
DBCC results for 'syscolumns'.
There are 3227 rows in 41 pages for object 'syscolumns'.
DBCC results for 'systypes'.
There are 24 rows in 1 pages for object 'systypes'.
DBCC results for 'syscomments'.
There are 1318 rows in 499 pages for object 'syscomments'.
DBCC results for 'sysfiles1'.
There are 2 rows in 1 pages for object 'sysfiles1'.
DBCC results for 'syspermissions'.
There are 580 rows in 2 pages for object 'syspermissions'.
DBCC results for 'sysusers'.
There are 13 rows in 1 pages for object 'sysusers'.
DBCC results for 'sysdepends'.
There are 3660 rows in 18 pages for object 'sysdepends'.
DBCC results for 'sysreferences'.
There are 0 rows in 1 pages for object 'sysreferences'.
DBCC results for 'sysfulltextcatalogs'.
There are 0 rows in 1 pages for object 'sysfulltextcatalogs'.
DBCC results for 'sysdatabases'.
There are 6 rows in 1 pages for object 'sysdatabases'.
DBCC results for 'sysxlogins'.
There are 4 rows in 1 pages for object 'sysxlogins'.
DBCC results for 'sysdevices'.
There are 6 rows in 1 pages for object 'sysdevices'.
DBCC results for 'sysmessages'.
There are 2997 rows in 122 pages for object 'sysmessages'.
DBCC results for 'sysconfigures'.
There are 43 rows in 1 pages for object 'sysconfigures'.
DBCC results for 'sysservers'.
There are 1 rows in 1 pages for object 'sysservers'.
DBCC results for 'syslanguages'.
There are 24 rows in 2 pages for object 'syslanguages'.
DBCC results for 'syscharsets'.
There are 105 rows in 30 pages for object 'syscharsets'.
DBCC results for 'sysaltfiles'.
There are 2 rows in 1 pages for object 'sysaltfiles'.
DBCC results for 'sysfilegroups'.
There are 1 rows in 1 pages for object 'sysfilegroups'.
DBCC results for 'sysallocations'.
```

```
There are 1 rows in 1 pages for object 'sysallocations'.
DBCC results for 'spt_committab'.
There are 0 rows in 1 pages for object 'spt_committab'.
DBCC results for 'spt_monitor'.
There are 1 rows in 1 pages for object 'spt_monitor'.
DBCC results for 'spt_values'.
There are 675 rows in 8 pages for object 'spt_values'.
DBCC results for 'spt_fallback_db'.
There are 0 rows in 1 pages for object 'spt_fallback_db'.
DBCC results for 'spt_fallback_dev'.
There are 0 rows in 1 pages for object 'spt_fallback_dev'.
.......
CHECKFILEGROUP found 0 allocation errors and 0 consistency errors in
database 'master'.
DBCC execution completed. If DBCC printed error messages, contact your
system administrator.
```

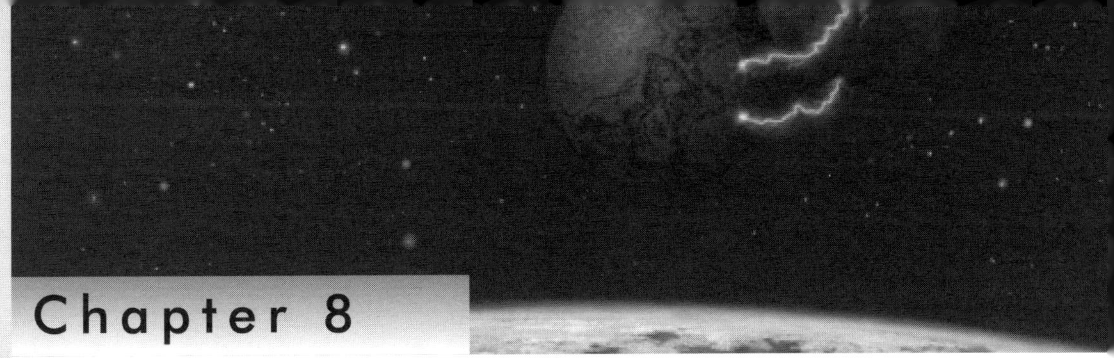

Chapter 8

Backing Up and Restoring Your Database

The adage, "Be prepared," that you heard from your grandmother years ago definitely applies here. Disasters tend to happen at the worst possible time (like just a few hours before your long-dreamed-of vacation or an important holiday or family event). This will be the moment your database system will fail and ruin all of your plans. Often corporations (of all sizes) do not create effective backup procedures.

Database Backups

A database backup is a full copy of all of the data in the database. This is typically performed at the end of the business day in order to capture data that reflects an entire day's work. You may want to back up more or less often based upon your own business needs. After the backups (one for each database) have been completed, and the integrity of the backup has been verified, get the backups off-site (home, safety deposit box, anywhere it will not be affected by a disaster at work). Note that you do not want all copies of your most recent backup off-site. A disaster during the day should not send you home looking for the prior evening's backup. It is also important to be able to replace the tape drive, if it goes bad, as well as whatever software you use for backup.

There are many different media to choose from, including writeable CD-ROMs, floppy disks, tapes, Zip drives, and Jaz drives. You may pick a particular media dependent on hardware you have already purchased, or you may choose based on price, amount of data that can be held on the media, or other personal factors. You may back up your database to one or as many tapes as needed, based upon the size of your database.

Drive Type/Cost*	Storage Medium/Cost*	Capacity*
Floppy disk/$100	Floppy disks/10 for $6	1.44 megabytes
CD-ROM drive/ $300-$400	CD/$1-$1.50	600 megabytes
Tape drive/$300-$3000 (price varies for storage capacity and vendor)	Tape cartridge/$2-$20	8-40 gigabytes
Jaz drive/$300	Jaz cartridge/$90	1 gigabyte
Zip drive/$200	Zip cartridge/$15	100 megabytes

** This table shows pricing and capacity for a variety of backup media. The information was current in December 1999. Note that prices drop seemingly daily.*

As you can see, for a small investment you can purchase a great insurance policy against data loss.

Backup Types

There are two backup types:

- **Complete Backup**—This is the most important. To run a full database backup you must use the *backup database* command. It is used to make a full copy of the entire database. It backs up all of the tables including your transaction log (note that this does not clean out your transaction log—see Chapter 9 for more information.) This backup must be performed prior to a differential backup because the differential backup only copies changes that have been made since this backup.

- **Differential Backup**—To do this you run the *backup transaction* command (or choose differential backup in Enterprise Manager). It will make a copy of your transaction log, which contains all modifications to the database. After copying the log to the backup media, this command clears the transaction log of any information no longer needed (permanent changes to the database), unless your database option Truncate log on checkpoint is selected. This option must be selected to keep the transaction log from filling up, which will cause all data modification statements to stop executing until you clear the log. You can use the sp_dboption command from the Query Analyzer to see what database options are turned on.

Backup Strategy

Now that we have covered the basics of backups, we will develop a comprehensive backup strategy.

First, we create a list of all of the logs, tables, and databases that should be backed up daily. These include:

- All user databases
- The master database
- Transaction log (remember—the transaction log fills up and must be cleaned out)

Note: Be sure to date/time stamp your backup media before you start your backup. It's stressful to need to restore from backup and not know which tape is the right one.

You should verify the success of the backup before you can be assured that the backup is complete. To be sure that your backup media is healthy, restore your database to a test area. A successful restore equals a good media backup. Remember, tapes and storage devices can be faulty, and you do not always know this until you try to read the device.

SQL Server (depending on your database size) will allow you to store more than one backup on a backup device. However, for simplicity, we suggest you use a one-to-one system (one database, one disk). If you really want multiple database backups on a single backup media, here is the procedure you need to follow:

1. For the first backup, initialize the tape but do not rewind (this gets the tape ready).
2. Back up the second database.
3. Back up the third database.
4. Rewind or record over the original backup.

Syntax (if you are not using Enterprise Manager):

```
backup database CustomerDB "Tape 1" volume = CustVol1 with init
backup database ProductionDB to Tape 1 volume = ProdVol1/* nounload is
the default */backup database SecurityDB to tape 1 volume = SecVol1
with unload
```

SQL Server Enterprise Manager allows you to choose Append to media, thus allowing you to do graphically the same work that we just went through one step at a time. This is a great option to use for something like the differential backups, but when you are performing a complete backup, use one media per backup.

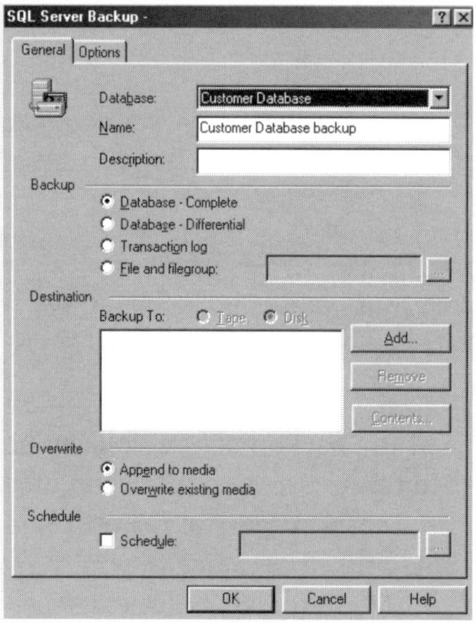

Another nice feature of SQL Server is that it automatically detects the media capacity of your backup device. This makes it harder to make a mistake. There was a time you specified the size, and you wrote that much to the tape whether the tape would hold the data or not.

Backup Approach

Backing up the individual databases is only one step of the complete backup procedure. The process should include all of the following steps to ensure a functional, thorough backup.

1. Standardize your backup procedures.
2. Back up your database.
   a. Back up the transaction log (only needs to be done if syslogs is located on a different device).
   b. Check your tape by restoring the database.
3. Back up the master database.
   a. Check the media (tape or disk) by restoring the database.

Standardizing Your Backup Procedures

There are some things to consider that are just from a pure business process perspective. Share your strategy so that someone else in your office understands it and knows how to complete the backups. They also should be able to follow the same procedure for labeling and getting the backups off-site. Make sure that the location of the backups is known. This assures your ability to have an uninterrupted vacation some day. You may want to post a schedule (see the following table) that works for your office. The schedule should describe the frequency with which you need to back up your logs and the databases.

Who	When	Frequency of Backups	Naming Standards	Which Databases	Types of Backups	How	Location
Identify responsible party	Date/Time	Schedule backups	Define standards for: Media labeling Database naming Device naming	List all databases	Database and transaction log backups	Disk or file devices	Where are the physical media copies?

You may want to include a rotation schedule for reusing your backup media. You will have to decide how far you need to track backups. In most shops, a one-week rotation should work well. However, you have to decide on the volatility of your site and what works for you.

Who	When	Backups	How	Device
Barney	M_W_F 4:00	customer	Striped multi tape	cd
	M_W_F 4:00	master	not striped, single tape	tape
	Every 4 hours	transaction log	Appended single tape in one-day intervals	files

Create a naming convention for your media backups. For example, you will want to include the name of the database, date, time, and possibly a notation of who created the backup(Customer Database/December 15, 1999/5:05 pm—Joe) or use the volume naming convention especially for tapes that you plan on appending (CustomerDB December 15 Dec 20). Then name your database backups so that they can easily be found on the tape CustomerDB December 17. Consistency in your naming conventions helps other people remember what to do and gets the tasks done faster. It also helps the recovery process along when/if a disaster strikes and you have to restore your database.

Backing Up the Databases

You can use SQL Enterprise Manager to back up your database.

1. Click the **Start** button.
2. Select **Programs**.
3. Select **Microsoft SQL Server 7.0**.
4. Select **Enterprise Manager**.

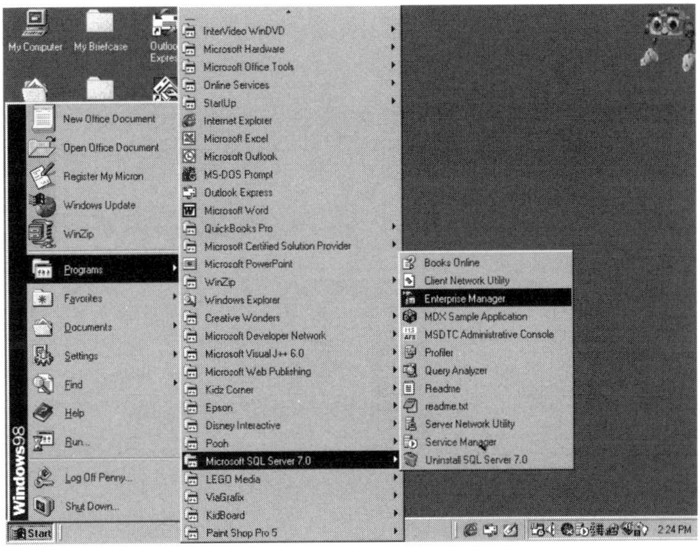

5. Open your server folder and then the **Databases** file. You will see your databases come up on the right side.

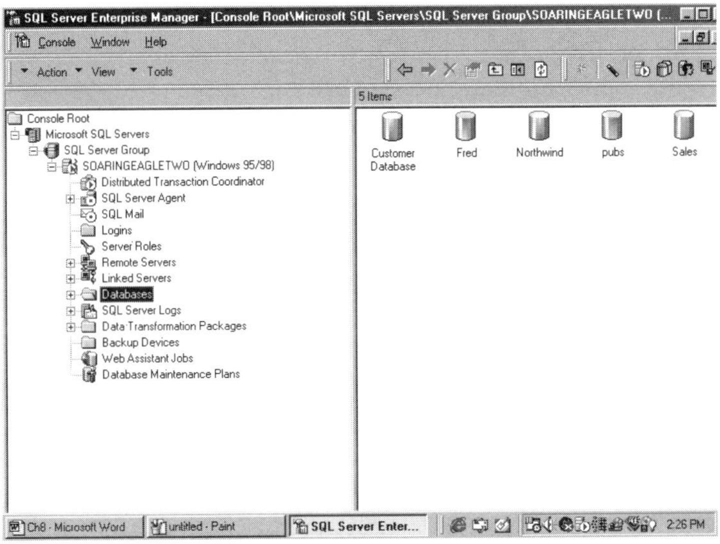

6. Right-click the database you want to back up. Select **Tools|Backup Database**.

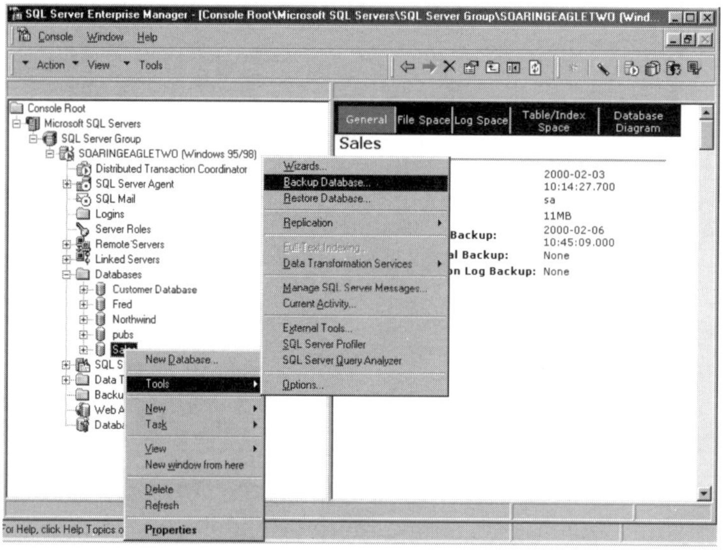

Notice on the SQL Server Backup dialog that the name of your database automatically appears, along with any description you may have entered at the time you built your database. Enterprise Manager gives you two choices of backups: complete (full backup of your database and logs) and differential (only a backup of the transaction log). At this time, we will choose the Complete backup option.

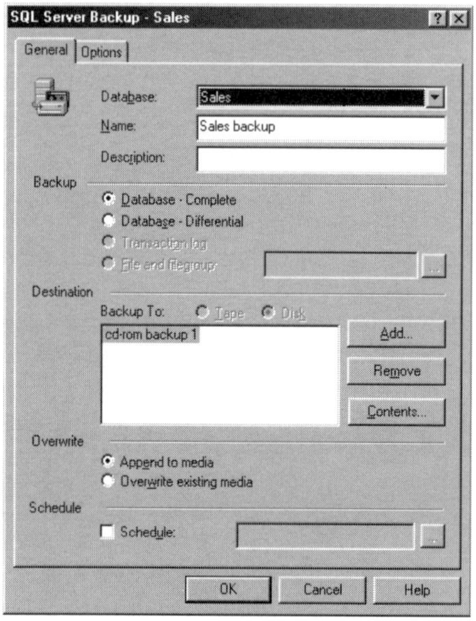

Overwrite Option

Append to media means that you would like SQL Server to search for the end of the old database backup and add the new backup onto the same media.

Overwrite means that you would like to use the whole media space again. This will cause an error if you have set an expiration date or time period on that media and the date or time period has not elapsed. This is a good thing; it helps us with our human flaws that come with overwork and fatigue. We recommend that you overwrite each time, and age out your backups manually.

Schedule Option

This option will allow you to schedule your backups and automate this process. Don't forget to install a new media and label it. However, the rest can be automated for you. This is a nice way to perform your backups overnight. Check the Schedule box, then click the button with the ellipsis (next to the Schedule text box) to see more detailed options.

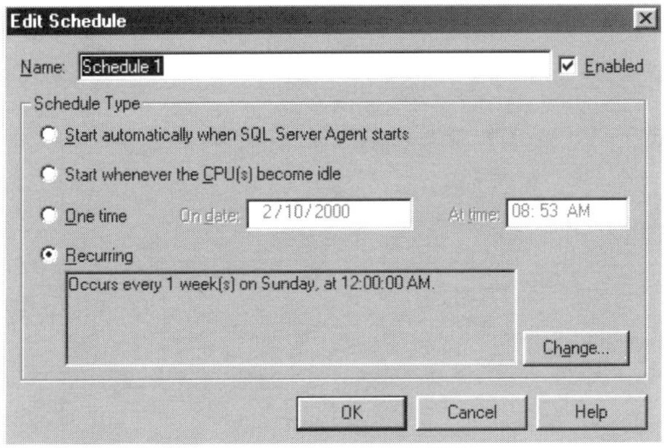

Under Schedule Type, you will see many options:

Start automatically when Server Agent starts
: The full use of Server Agent is covered in Chapter 13. It is a tool which can be directed to watch certain occurrences in your database and sends alarms to you to notify you of a pending problem or occurrence.

Start whenever the CPU(s) become idle
: You may want to use this option to back up the transaction log at several points in a day. If you use this option, though, you will still have to watch the transaction log as it fills throughout the day.

One time
: This option is just what it sounds like.

Recurring

Under the Recurring option is a text box. Next to the text box is a button labeled Change. If you want to select a backup to occur daily, weekly, or monthly, you click on the Change button and set those backup intervals for yourself.

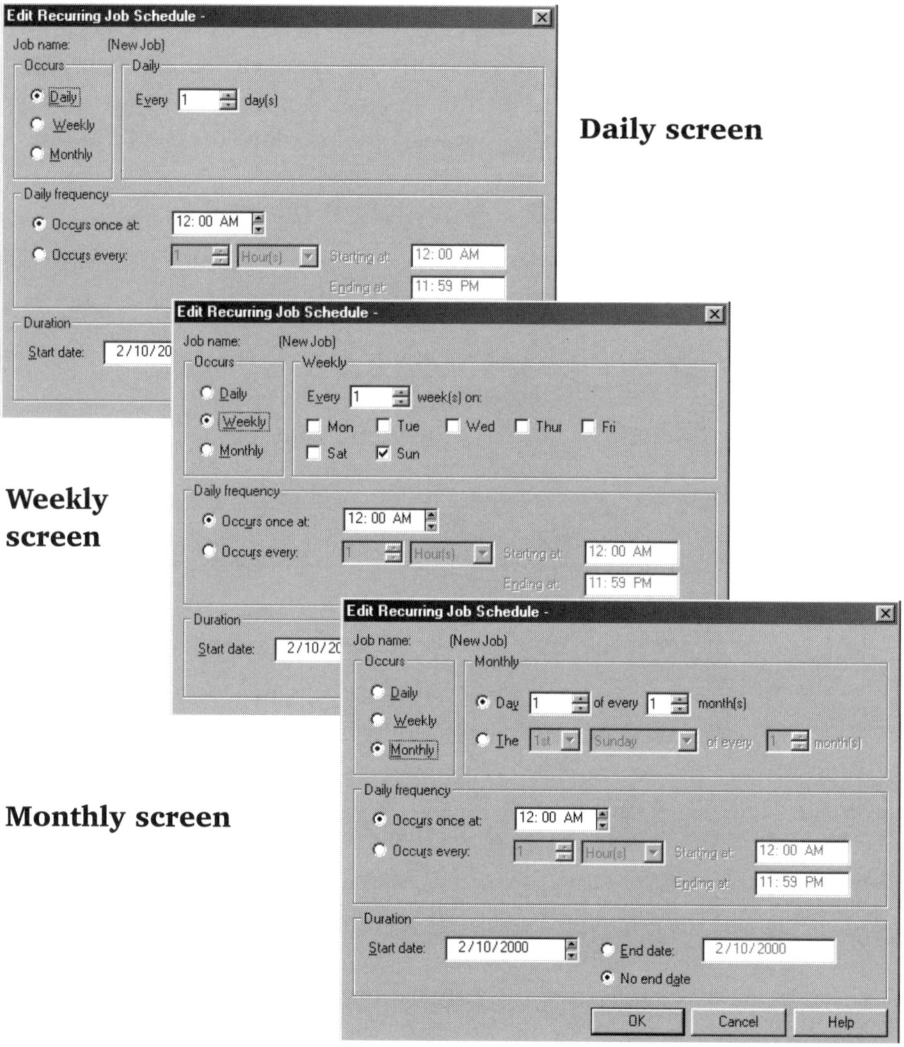

For all of the interval choices, you are able to enter the hour and duration start and end dates. Select a backup plan that fits your needs.

Adding Your Backup Device

In the SQL Server Backup dialog you will be able to add your backup device (if you have not done this previously). To do this:

1. Click the **Add** button under Destination. The Choose Backup Destination dialog box appears.

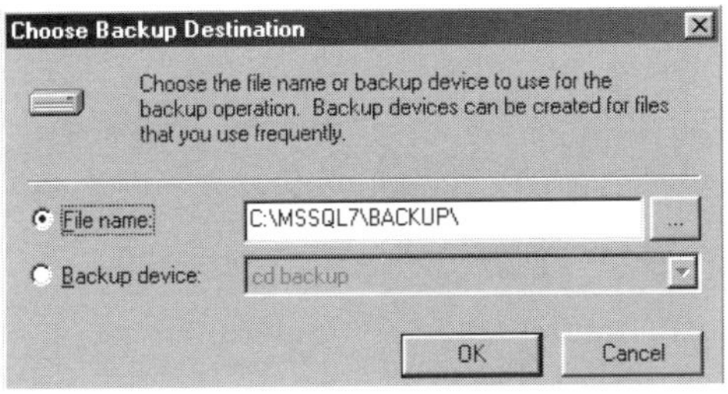

2. Click **Backup device**, then click on the down arrow in the drop-down list, and select **<New Backup Device>**.

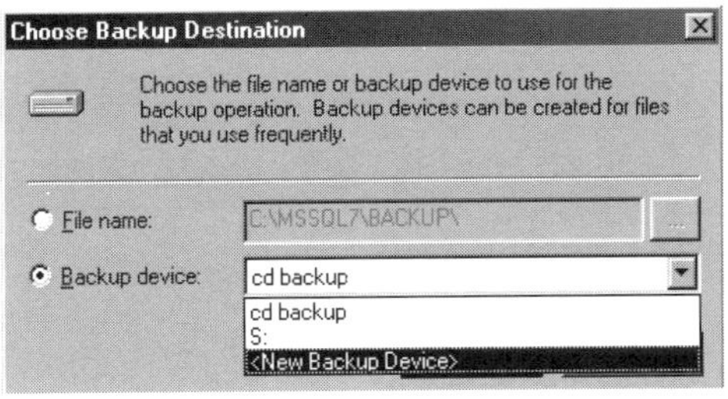

The next screen that pops up is the Backup Device Properties—New Device screen.

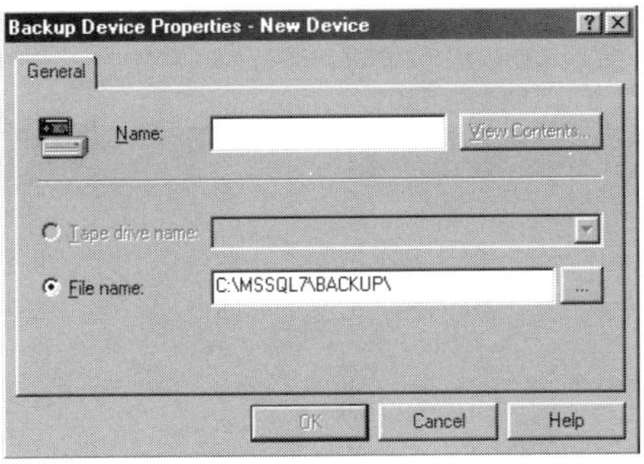

3. Enter the name of your device and file location in the Name and File name fields. Click **OK**. You should get a message that says, "Your new device has been created successfully." Now click **OK** on the next screen.

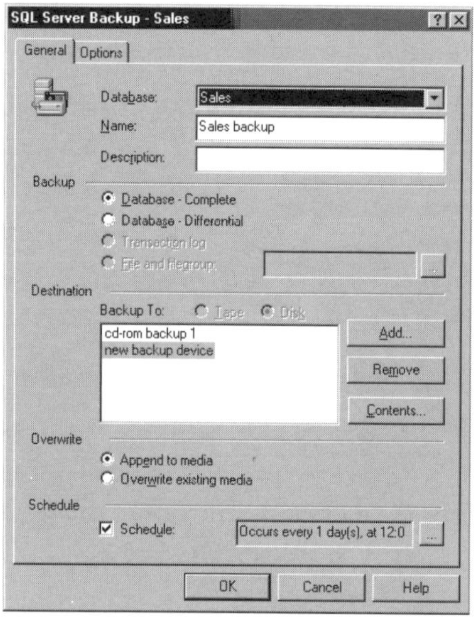

You should see your new device in the backup list. At the top of the screen you will see an Options tab. Click on that tab.

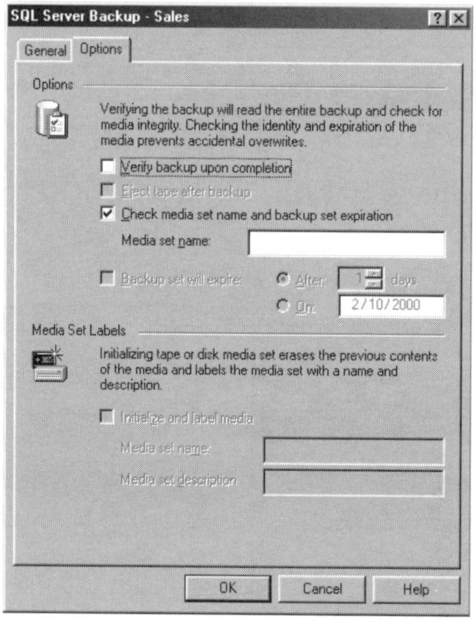

This is a very useful dialog. Here you can do many things to make restoring easier. Check Verify backup upon completion to give you that comfortable feeling of a job successfully completed. Then be sure to use the Check media set name and backup set expiration option so that SQL Server will help you with your tape rotations and help eliminate human error.

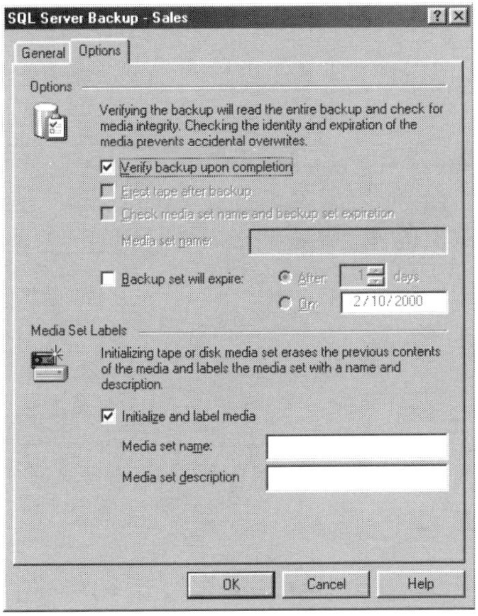

Note: If you select Append to media on the General tab, the Check media set name and backup set expiration option will be turned off. Therefore, you should double-check your media name tag before you overwrite your media.

When you click OK at this point your database backup will begin. Then if you have selected Verify backup upon completion your SQL Server will notify you of a successful backup.

A Behind-the-Scenes Look: Database Backups

SQL Server Enterprise Manager is actually performing some programming functions for you automatically. The following information will give you a little insight as to what is happening and help you to develop as a systems administrator by learning methods you should follow to get more information from your database.

Step 1: Back Up the Database

You use the *backup database* command to make a full copy of your database. The simplified syntax for this command is:

```
Backup database {dbname | @dbname_var}
  TO backup_device [, backup_device[. . . , backup_device32]]
[WITH options
[[,] STATS [ = percentage]]]
where
backup_device =
{backup_device_name \ @backup_device_namevar}
\ {DISK | TAPE \ FLOPPY |PIPE} =
{temp_backup_device' | @tempp_backup_+device_var}}
[VOLUME == {volid | @volid_var}]
options =
[[,] {UNLOAD | NOUNLOAD}]
[[,] {INIT | NOINIT}]
[[,] {SKIP | NOSKIP}]
[[,] {{EXPIREDATE =  {date | @date_var}}
| {RETAINDAYS = {days | @days_var}}]
```

The following table describes the parameters used in the Full database backup syntax.

Parameter	Description
dbname	The name of the database you are attempting to back up.
backup_device	The backup device that is defined with sp_addbackupdevice or you can directly specify a disk or tape device when you are striping them.
RETAINDAYS = days	An option used for any backup device. It keeps the backup from being overwritten until a specific amount of time has passed.
EXPIREDATE date	Actually, this option is a toggle button in SQL Enterprise Manager which does not allow a backup to be overwritten until the date has passed.
STATS = percentage	Returns the percentage of pages backed up in increments specified by the value of the percentage. If the percentage is not specified, SQL Server automatically shows the statistics in 10% increments.

Listed below are the options used in the Full database backup syntax and their descriptions.

VOLUME	Labels your backup, which can be specified during a load onto your media; for example, a value for volume as a concatenation of your database name and the date (CustomerDB_Mar02). If your backup media contains backups from Mar 01–05, then by using VOLUME you will be able to find the backup that you want.
UNLOAD | NOUNLOAD	Controls the rewinding of the tape. NOUNLOAD should be used unless this is the last backup you want on the tape.
INIT | NOINIT	Determines whether the backup will be appended to the tape or the entire tape volume will be reinitialized. You use INIT when backing up the first time to a tape; you use NOINIT to allow for multiple backups to a single tape.
SKIP | NOSKIP	Indicates whether ANSI tape labels are read (NOSKIP) or ignored (SKIP). When SKIP is specified and the ANSI label of a tape warns that it has expired or that you don't have permission to write to it, SQL Server will ignore the warning. If the tape on which you are writing is new then SQL Server writes a new label on the first try. NOSKIP tells the SQL Server to read the warnings. The default is NOSKIP.

Step 2: Back Up the Transaction Log

You may want to back up the transaction log more often than executing a full database backup. Backing up the transaction log in Enterprise Manager is called a differential backup. This option is given to you on your Backup Database tool in SQL Enterprise Manager. Because the log will grow until it is truncated, backing up the transaction log (to truncate unused transactions) is very important to remember.

To perform a differential backup, right-click the database you want to back up and select Tools|Backup Database from the pop-up menu.

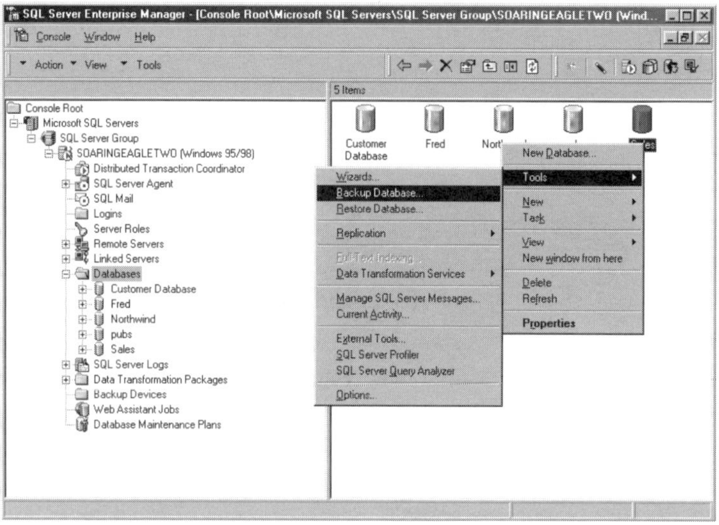

In the SQL Server Backup window, choose Database-Differential under Backup instead of Database-Complete like we did earlier in this chapter.

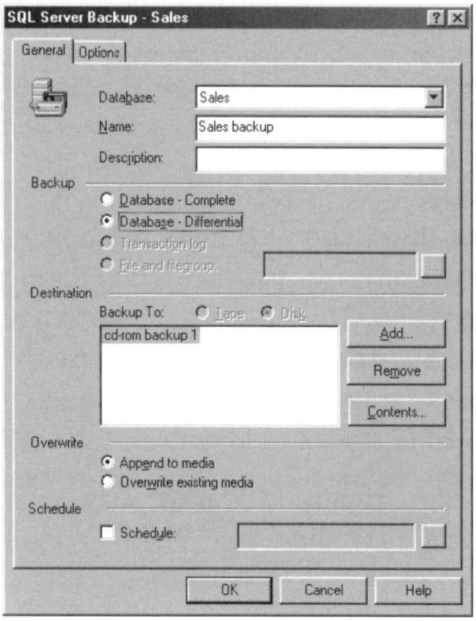

Just as when performing a complete backup, you will not have the ability to set the same options on all of the tabs. You only need to keep your differential backups until your next complete backup. For example, if you back up the transaction log three times a day, you need only keep those three differential backups.

We recommend that you track your transaction log to be sure that it has not filled. Remember the SQL Server will pause when the transaction log is full. SQL Server Enterprise Manager will find the transaction log that coincides with the database that you are in. If the log fills, all transactions will stop until space is made for the log. To track the transaction log and to understand more details about the transaction log, please refer to Chapter 9.

A Behind-the-Scenes Look: Transaction Log Backups

The transaction log backup copies to your backup media all changes that have been logged to the database. Along the way, it also cleans out all of these completed transactions from the log. This is the normal way that you empty out a transaction log in a production database (see Chapter 9 for a more detailed discussion). To back up the transaction database name to devicename, use the following code:

```
BACKUP TRANSACTION {dbname | @dbname_var}
[To dump_device [, dump_device2 [..., dump_device32]]]
[WITH [TRUNCATE_ONLY | NO_LOG | NO_TRUNCATE}
{options}]
where
dump_device =
{dump_device_name | @dump_device_name_var}
| {DISK | TAPE | FLOPPY | PIPE} =
{'temp_dump_device' }}
[VOLUME = {volid | @volid_var}]
options=
[[, ] {UNLOAD | NOUNLOAD}]
[[,] {INIT | NOINIT}]
[[,] {SKIP | NOSKIP}]
[[,] {EXPIREDATE == {date | @date_var}}
| {RETAINDAYS = {days | @days_Var}}]
```

The Master Database

The master database is small. In fact, the default space allocation is only 17 megabytes. It is also not a very active database. However, if there is a master device failure, then not having a current backup of the master database can be traumatic; you will have to rebuild the entire server.

You need to back up this database whenever you are inserting or deleting rows in the system tables—in other words, any server activities like database creation or growth, option changes, adding users, defining new disks, etc. The master database does not have a separate log, so all backups are complete database backups.

Note: As a precaution, you should back up your master database as often as you back up your other databases. Place the master database on a single tape/disk alone. Do not stripe (putting a database backup on more than one device SQL Server can break up the database in equal portions and spread the data over 32 devices) the master database if at all possible. For most systems, the master database will fit on one backup medium so this should not be a problem.

Restoring Your Database

It is important to keep your cool when something goes wrong. Remember, you can't fall off the floor! (If you can, your problems are too severe for this book.) Focus on the steps required to solve the problem, and later decide if it was avoidable, to improve for the next time. Once something happens, the most important thing to do is to think, take a deep breath, and get your system up and running. It can happen to anybody. Just get started, restore your database, and get everyone back to work. You can restore your database by right-clicking on your database and choosing Tools|Restore Database.

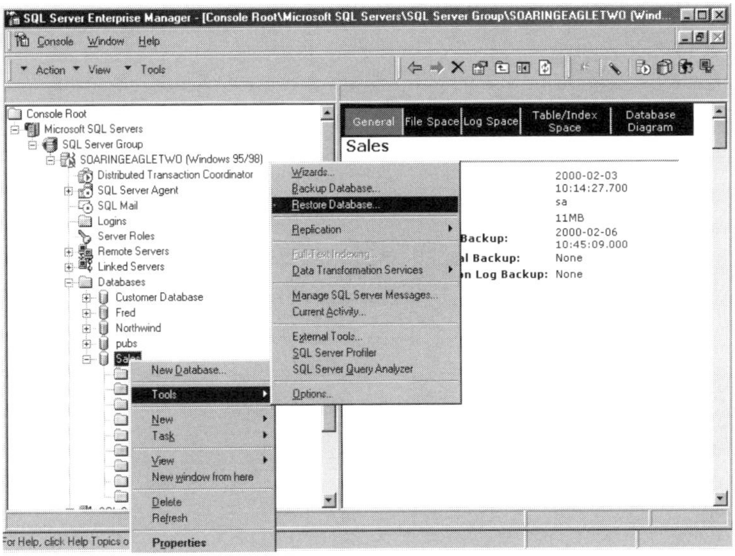

Since you have already selected your database, SQL Server Enterprise Manager can detect the database that you want to restore and determines whether you can apply a transaction log backup as well.

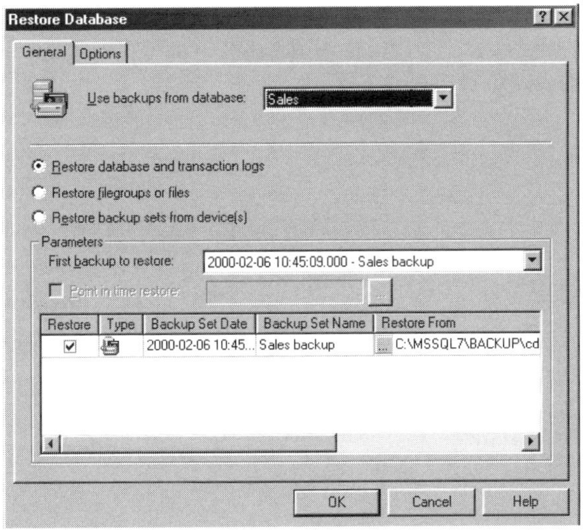

The SQL Server Enterprise Manager also automatically tells you when your restore has been successfully completed.

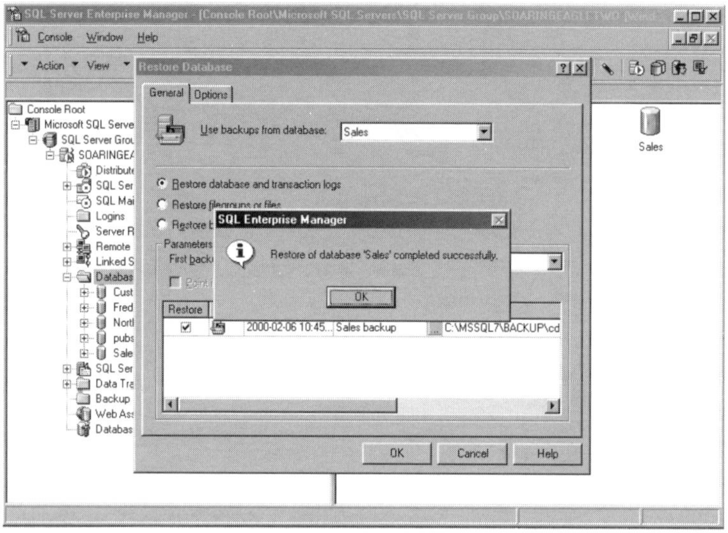

If a Disaster Has Struck

If a disaster has occurred, you may need to re-create the database. First, you will have to drop the corrupt database. Try this first by right-clicking on the database in the SQL Server Enterprise Manager, and highlighting Delete. If, for any reason, this does not work (sometimes, if a database is in an odd state, the server will not remove it normally), you can use the following syntax from SQL Profiler:

```
sp_dbremove database [ , dropdev]
```

Second, you must create a new database structure. To check to see if you have space available on your disk, click once on the drive, and you'll see disk information on the left:

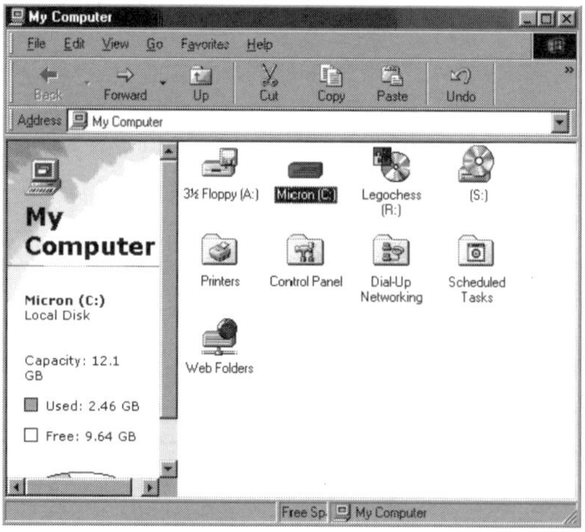

Access the Enterprise Manager, right-click on Databases, and select New Database from the pop-up menu.

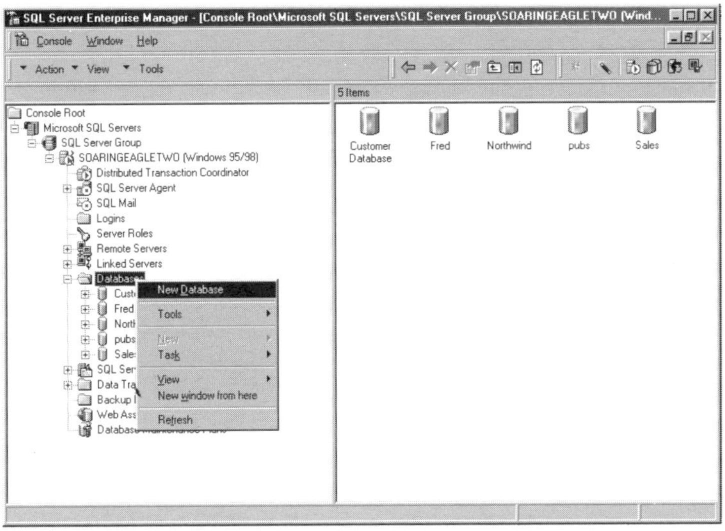

You'll need to enter your database name, where you'd like it to go, and an initial size. We recommend you check the Automatically grow file option. You can choose whether to do this in megabytes or by percent.

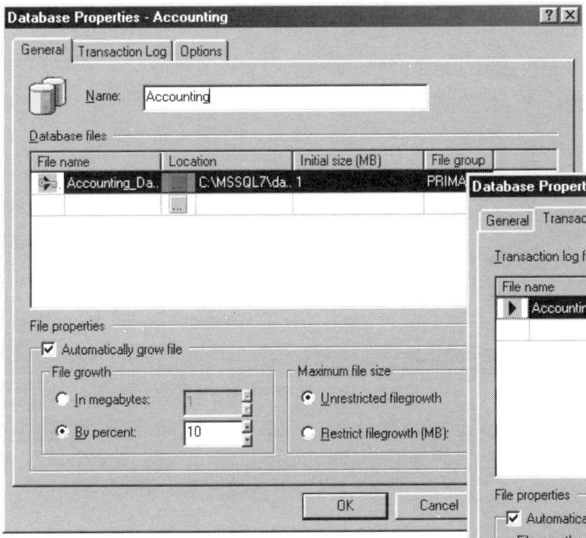

That is really all there is to it. You now have a database. Note that if the database is very large, this step may take a while.

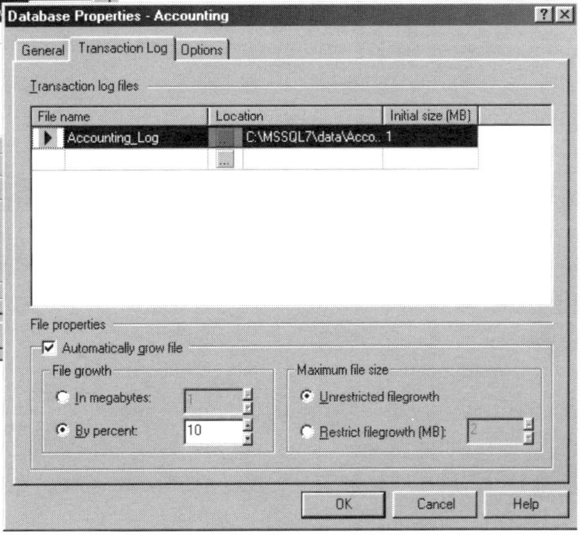

Chapter 9

Transaction Log Management

A transaction is defined among “techies” simply as a unit of work. More specifically, it is some amount of data processing that you want to have complete as a group or fail as a group. For example, you are at your ATM machine trying to get cash out. The machine will verify that you have money in your account to cover the cash withdrawal, subtract that amount from your account balance, and give you your money. But what happens if in between steps two and three, a squirrel chews through a transformer cable, and the power to the ATM goes out? Is your bank account still debited? When the power comes back on, do you suddenly get your cash? Or does it go to the fortunate person who was waiting for the power to come on, way after you left? In real life, you do not want steps two and three to be independent; you want them to be completely dependent. This is called a unit of work, or a transaction. The Microsoft SQL Server 7.0 transaction log exists for the purpose of making sure that not only does your transaction complete or fail as a unit, but everybody else’s transactions, potentially running at the same time, also complete or fail as a unit.

Truncating the Transaction Log

The transaction log, as you can imagine, will get large over time, because it records every change that is made to the data, so that nothing is ever partially completed. You, as a DBA, must make sure that the transaction log does not fill up. If it does, all data modification on your server will simply stop.

Remember that this section of the book is on database-specific maintenance, and that a transaction log is specific to a database. This means that if you are managing multiple databases on a server, you must do this for each. There are two basic ways of accomplishing this.

First, you can turn on the database option Truncate log on checkpoint. This will truncate all the inactive (completed and recorded on disk) transactions in your database transaction log. You can turn the option on like this:

1. Right-click the database and choose **Properties**.

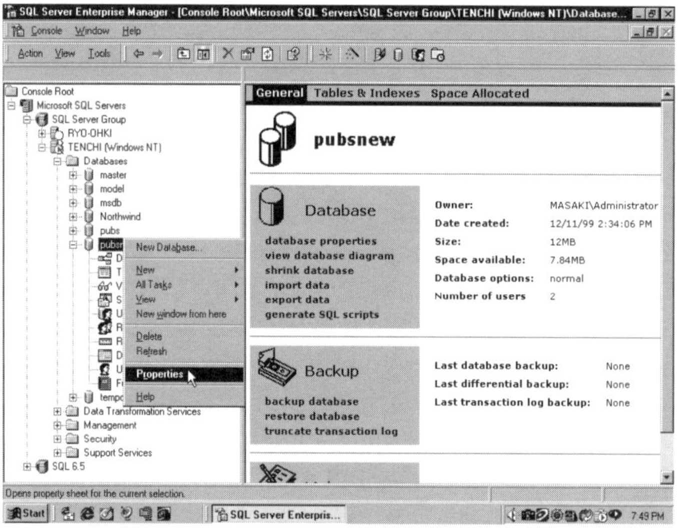

2. Select the **Options** tab in the Properties dialog.
3. Check **Truncate log on checkpoint**.

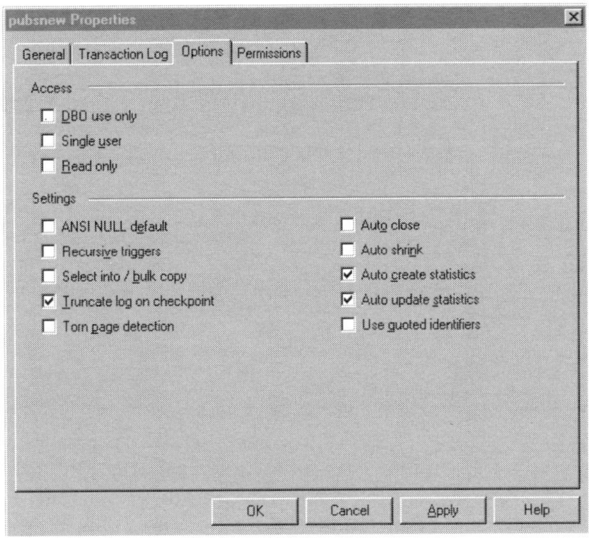

4. Click **OK**.

There is a downside to turning this on. Picture the following scenario: You backed up your database overnight. Everything has been going great all morning. Suddenly, mid-afternoon, you have a data corruption. What happens to all the work that was entered into the system all morning?

If you restore the database from a backup, you will overlay/replace/destroy/etc. your current database. A database restore is destructive to the old database. This means that you will have lost all the work from that morning. Your solution, then, before you load, is to do a differential backup. This stores all the changes from the database, and when you load the differential backup, those changes will be applied. If luck is with you, this differential backup may allow you to retain all the work you have done that morning. If you are truncating the log, however, there will be nothing there. So, if you want to be able to preserve the day's work (transactions) you do not want to turn that option on. Instead, you will go with option two, which is to maintain your transaction log.

You can find out how big your transaction log is like this:

1. Click on the appropriate database in the Enterprise Manager.
2. Click on the **Space Allocated** option in the taskpad.

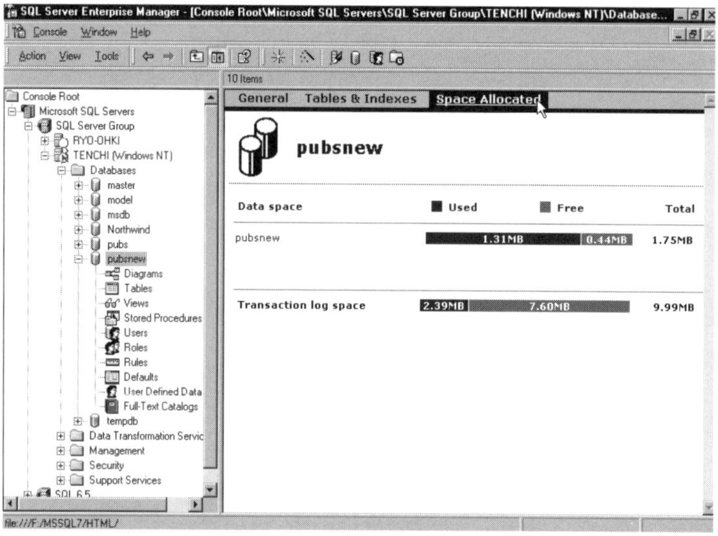

If your log is filling up, you have two options. The first is to perform a differential backup (see Chapter 8). This will empty out the log. As each log grows and fills, you can make additional incremental backups. The second option, preferred for small systems, is to simply make the log big enough to accommodate all the day's transactions, and then some. This way, if there is a corruption, you only have to take a current differential backup, restore the backup, and apply the differential backup. There is one catch: If you are not automatically truncating the log, you must do it manually. The database backup does not automatically truncate it. If the log does fill up, you need to truncate it to allow additional transactions to take place in the log. We suggest truncating the transaction log (perform a differential backup) right before you back up the database. So, initially, check the size of the transaction log during the day to make sure it does not fill. At the end of the day, note how full it is, and make sure it has room to accommodate twice as many transactions. Once a month or so, check again at the end of the day to make sure it's not nearing the point where it might fill up.

If you need to make the transaction log bigger, you can do it like this:

1. In the Enterprise Manager, right-click on the appropriate database and select **Properties**.
2. Select the **General** tab in the Properties dialog.
3. Click the **Database Properties** option.

4. Select the **Transaction Log** tab.

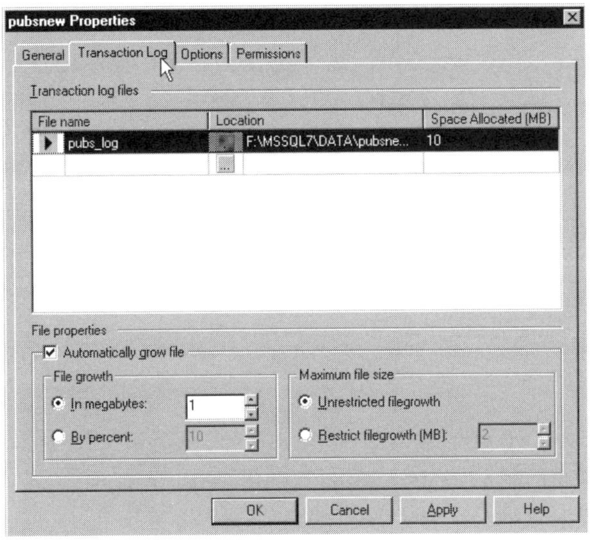

5. Click inside the Space Allocated (MB) box of a transaction log file and enter a larger number.

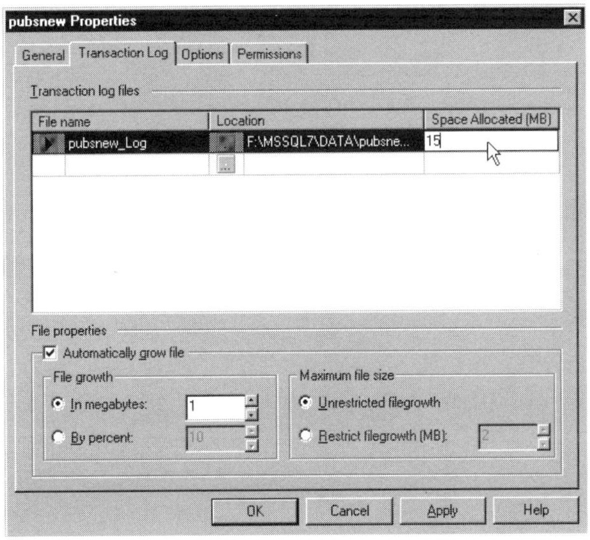

6. Click **OK**.

If you would like to get fancier, you can tell the log to automatically get bigger rather than fill up, like this:

1. In the Properties window, click on the **Transaction Log** tab.
2. Check the **Automatically grow file** option.

There are two options you can use to set automatic growth:

- **In megabytes** The transaction log file will increase by exactly the number of megabytes specified.
- **By percent** The transaction log file will increase by the percentage specified.

3. Click **OK**.

The basic things to remember here are to monitor the growth of your transaction log, make sure it doesn't fill, and decide how to manage it based on the needs of your business.

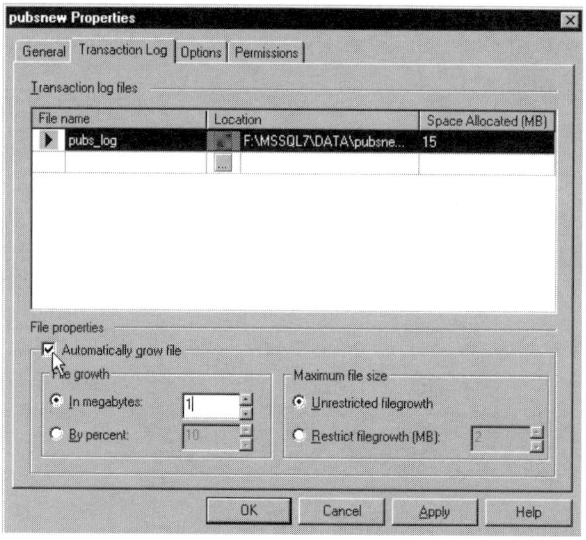

Chapter 10

Database Space Management

A database is not a physical thing that you can pick up, like a hard drive; it is an intangible thing, like data. From this perspective, the database is the thing that contains all of your data, which takes physical form in disks. A database usually starts out with a finite amount of space, and can be expanded manually or automatically.

Monitoring the Size of Your Database

You can check the size of your database like this:

1. In Enterprise Manger, click on the appropriate database.
2. Select **Space Allocated** in the taskpad.

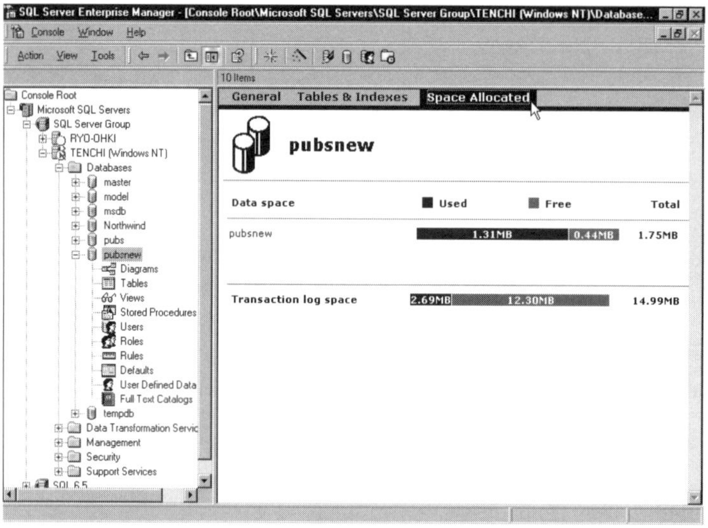

You can manually expand it like this:

1. In the Enterprise Manager, click on the appropriate database.
2. Select **General** in the taskpad.
3. Click on the **database properties** option.

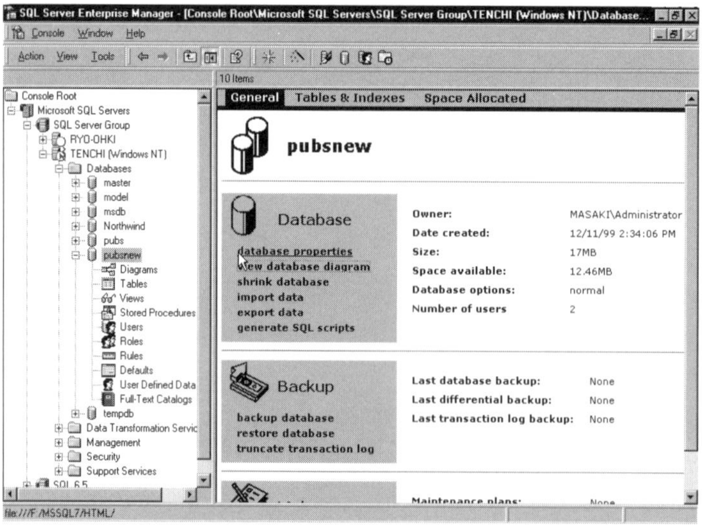

4. Select the **General** tab.

5. Click inside the Space Allocated (MB) box of a database file and enter a larger number.

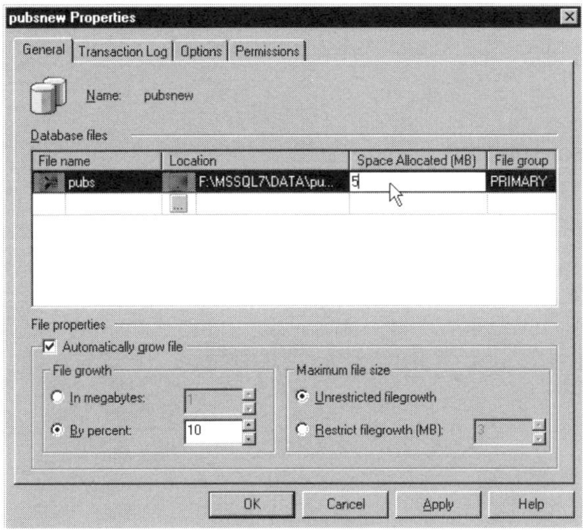

6. Click **OK**.

You can tell it to expand automatically like this:

1. Click on the **General** tab.
2. Check the **Automatically grow file** option.

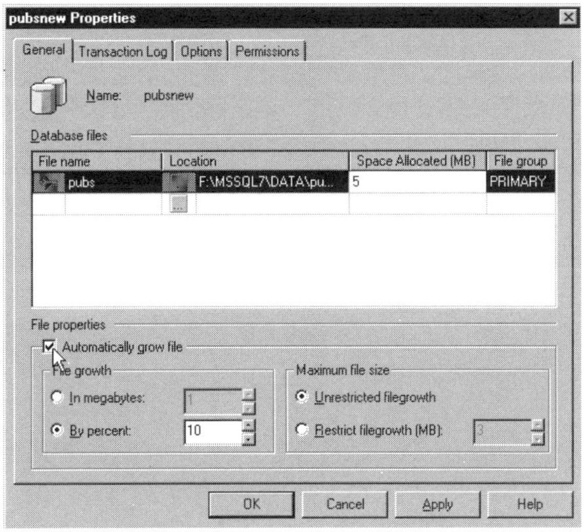

Note there are two options for automatic growth:

- **In megabytes** The file will be increased by exactly the number of megabytes specified.
- **By percent** The file will be increased by the percentage specified.

3. Click **OK**.

Now, here's where attention to detail is important: If the data fills up all the space in the database, and the database is not made bigger (manually or automatically), then you can no longer put data into your database. So, identify how full your database is by clicking Space Allocated in the taskpad.

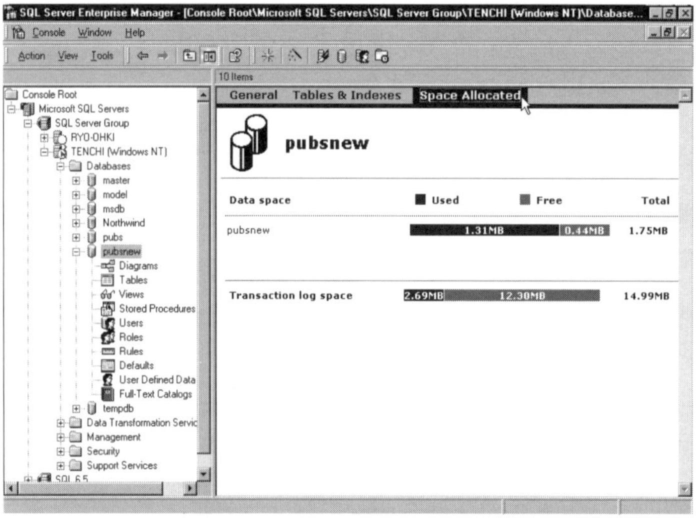

Every month or so, record how full your database is:

Month	Space Used	Space Available (Allocated)
January	50 MB	350 MB
February	75 MB	350 MB
March	100 MB	350 MB
April	150 MB	350 MB

In the previous chart, we seem to have a nice, smooth growth of about 25 MB of data per month. This should lead you to predict that you fill a 350 MB database in 350/25=14 months. That is a reasonable guess. But you need to check your results. Perhaps you took on additional clients, there was a cold and flu (or tax) season, or some other event that drives your data needs. In April, we used an additional 50 MB, not 25. Does that mean that you are going to use 50 MB more each month? Or go back to 25? The answer: You can't know. That is why you have to pay attention. Watch your database space utilization closely. Use these data to predict when you might need to buy more disk space. Then act based on hard data.

Chapter 11

Updating Index Statistics

Updating your index statistics is the single most important thing that you need to do in order to maintain performance in your database. With Microsoft SQL Server 7.0, this normally happens automatically. Under some circumstances, though, (when you are loading lots of data, for example) the automated statistics update may not be running often enough to keep your system performing smoothly. In this chapter, we look at the procedures for manually updating your index statistics.

The Cost-Based Optimizer

SQL Server has a cost-based optimizer. Let's take a moment and discuss what this means. When a query (request for data) is submitted (sent) to the server, there are a variety of methods the server may use to resolve the query (return the correct set of data). This ranges from a table scan (reading an entire table looking for the results) to using an existing index to creating an index automatically and dynamically (as you may guess, this is not efficient).

The *optimizer* is the software within the SQL Server which determines the best (read: fastest) approach to retrieving the data.

Cost-based means that the server evaluates all practical approaches to resolving the query, and uses that method.

How does the server determine the best method? Well, the answer to that question is itself a separate five-day class. The short answer is that the server breaks the query into a query tree and picks the best approach for each component of the tree based on its own internal statistics regarding the usefulness of each index. Like the table of contents in a book, statistics give the optimizer a place to start looking. If the statistics are missing, the optimizer must look at all the pages (as in the book). Worse, if the statistics are wrong, the optimizer must first follow the wrong path and subsequently look at all the pages in the book. You need to make sure that the SQL Server's optimizer has access to reasonably recent statistical information.

Commands

Historically, these statistics needed to be updated manually. With the advent of Microsoft SQL Server 7.0, the server can now do this automatically. If, however, you are experiencing seemingly inexplicable performance problems, or if you are loading a lot of data or your initial data, you may need to instruct the server to update statistics for the table(s) involved. Here are the commands and system procedures that you can use to maintain your statistics pages:

UPDATE STATISTICS	The base command which instructs the server to reset the information for a particular table or for a table's index.
SP_AUTOSTATS	Enables or disables the automatic statistics settings for a particular table or one or more of its indexes.
SP_UPDATESTATS	This command is your friend. It runs UPDATE STATISTICS against all of the tables in a database.
CREATE STATISTICS	Allows you to create the statistical information for columns that are not in indexes.
DROP STATISTICS	Removes statistics created by the CREATE STATISTICS command.
DBCC SHOW_STATISTICS	Retrieves and shows statistics for a specific table and index combination.

UPDATE STATISTICS

This command reinitializes the distribution of key values (statistics) for the specified table. It is run automatically when an index is created on a table that already contains data (so you do not need to run this command if you are dropping and rebuilding indexes).

Syntax

```
UPDATE STATISTICS table
[
index
| (statistics_name[,...n])
]
[ WITH
[
[FULLSCAN]
| SAMPLE number {PERCENT | ROWS}]
]
[[,] [ALL | COLUMNS | INDEX]
[[,] NORECOMPUTE]
]
```

Arguments

table
: The name of the table for which to update statistics. Index names are not unique within a database (though they are unique for a table), so you must specify the table name even if you are only updating the statistics for an index. We recommend, however, that you only update statistics for an entire table.

index
: This is the index for which statistics are being updated (unless of course this is for all indexes on a table).

statistics_name
: If you are going to create a set of statistics for non-indexed columns, this is where you can update those statistics independently.

n

This is a placeholder indicating that multiple statistics_name groups can be specified.

FULLSCAN

Specifies that all rows in the table should be read to gather the statistics (rather than a random sampling). Using FULLSCAN is the same as using SAMPLE 100 PERCENT, but it cannot be used with the SAMPLE option.

SAMPLE number {PERCENT | ROWS}

This specifies the percentage of the table or the number of rows to sample when collecting statistics for larger tables. If the PERCENT, ROWS, or number option results in too few rows being sampled, SQL Server automatically corrects the sampling based on the number of existing rows in the table.

The default behavior is to perform a sample scan on the target table, with the SQL Server automatically calculating the optimal sample size.

ALL | COLUMNS | INDEX

This specifies whether the UPDATE STATISTICS statement affects column statistics, index statistics, or all existing statistics. If no option is specified (recommended), the UPDATE STATISTICS statement affects all statistics. Only one type (ALL, COLUMNS, or INDEX) can be specified for each UPDATE STATISTICS statement.

NORECOMPUTE

Specifies that statistics that become out of date are not automatically recomputed. Don't do this. Statistics become out of date depending on the number of INSERT, UPDATE, and DELETE operations performed on indexed columns. When specified, this option causes SQL Server to disable automatic statistics rebuilding. To restore automatic statistics recomputation, you will have to reissue the UPDATE STATISTICS command without the NORECOMPUTE option or execute SP_AUTOSTATS.

The UPDATE STATISTICS command should be run in the SQL Server Query Analyzer:

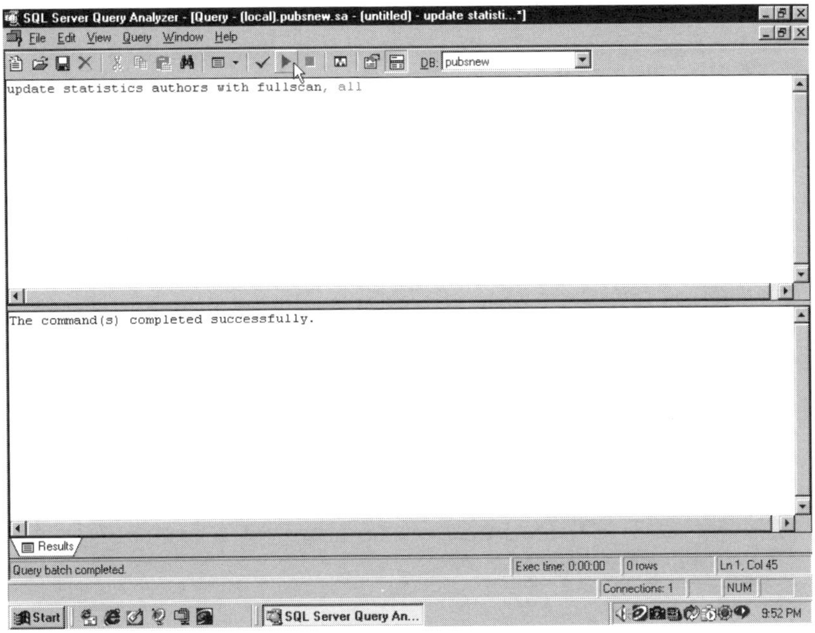

SP_AUTOSTATS

This is how you change the way statistics are automatically managed. SP_AUTOSTATS will display or change the automatic UPDATE STATISTICS setting for a specific index or all indexes (recommended) for a given table in the current database.

Syntax

```
sp_autostats [@tblname =] 'table_name'
[, [@flagc =] 'stats_flag']
[, [@indname =] 'index_name']
```

Arguments

[@tblname =] 'table_name'

This is the name of the table for which we will display or change the automatic UPDATE STATISTICS setting. If index_name is also supplied, SQL Server enables the automatic UPDATE STATISTICS setting for that index.

[@flagc =] 'stats_flag'
: This sets the automatic UPDATE STATISTICS setting for the specified table to enabled (ON) or disabled (OFF).

[@indname =] 'index_name'
: This is the name of the index for which to enable or disable the automatic UPDATE STATISTICS setting.

Note that a stored procedure can be called with or without the parameter names.

This statement:

```
EXEC sp_autostats authors, 'OFF', au_id
```

is equivalent to this statement:

```
EXEC sp_autostats @tblname = authors, @flagc ='OFF', @indname = au_id
```

The SP_AUTOSTATS procedure should be run in the SQL Server Query Analyzer.

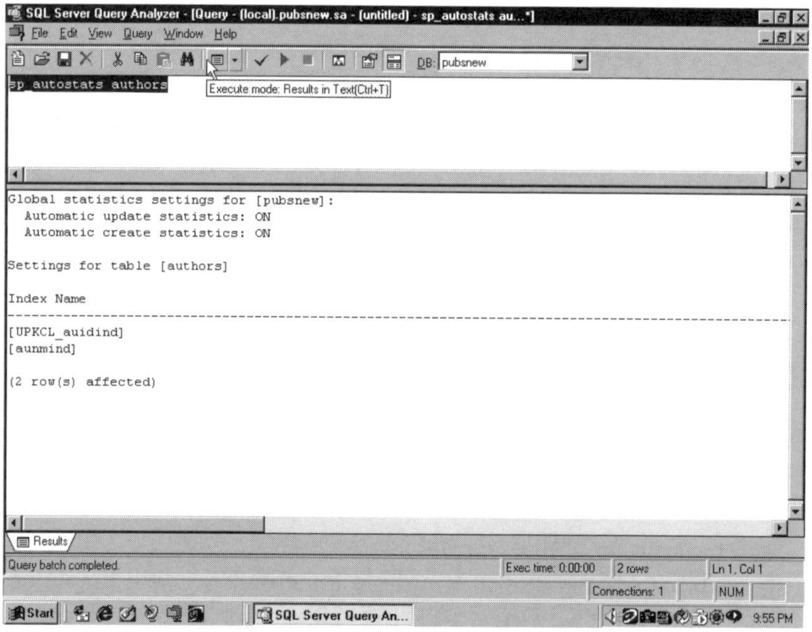

SP_UPDATESTATS

This command is your friend if you are manually running UPDATE STATISTICS. It will run the UPDATE STATISTICS command on all user-defined tables in the current database. In the old days, we used to have to do these one at a time. This procedure builds a dynamic list, and executes it.

Syntax

```
sp_updatestats
```

The SP_UPDATESTATS command displays messages indicating its progress. When the update is completed, it reports that statistics have been updated for all tables.

The SP_UPDATESTATS command should be run in the Query Analyzer.

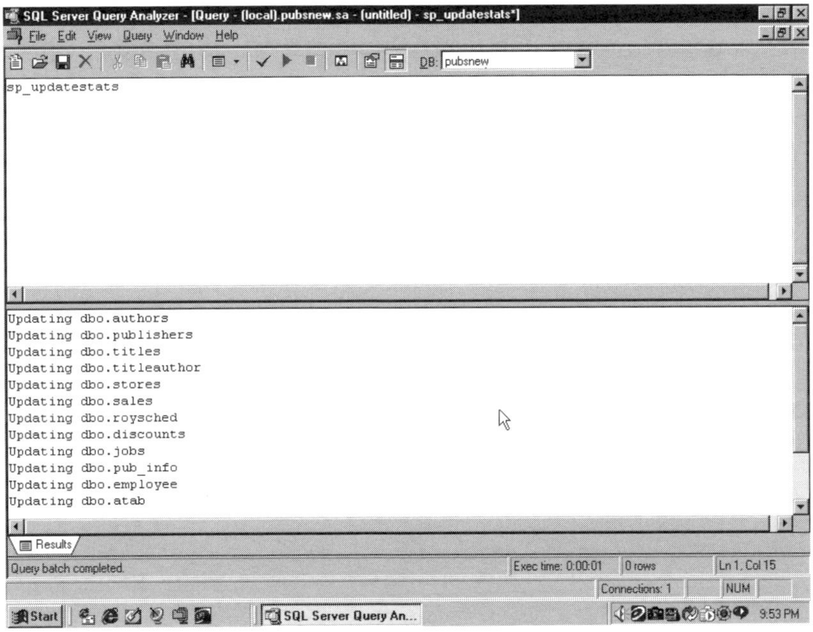

DBCC SHOW_STATISTICS

For true geeks (like your authors), this command is fun because it shows you what the optimizer knows about your data. It displays the current distribution statistics for the specified target index on the specified table.

Syntax

```
DBCC SHOW_STATISTICS (table, target)
```

Arguments

table
: This is the name of the table for which to display statistics information.

target
: This is the name of the index for which to display statistics information.

The results returned indicate the selectivity of an index (this means the level of uniqueness, or lack of) which provides the basis for determining whether or not an index is useful to the optimizer. To see the last date the statistics were updated, you can use STATS_DATE. Here is an example of a query that uses STATS_DATE:

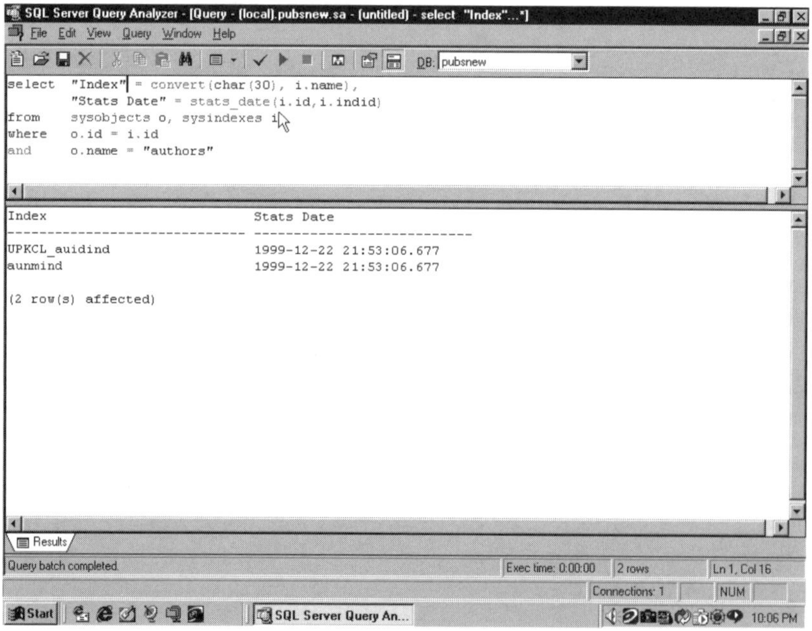

DBCC SHOW_STATISTICS should be run in the SQL Server Query Analyzer and produces results similar to this sample output:

```
dbcc show_statistics (authors, aunmind)
------------------------------
Statistics for INDEX 'aunmind'.
Updated              Rows Rows Sampled Steps   Density  Average key length
-------------------- ---- ------------------   ------   -----------------
Dec 22 1999 9:53PM   23   23                   23       4.3478262E-2
                                                        24.52174

(1 row(s) affected)
All density      Columns
------------     --------------------------
4.5454547E-2     au_lname
4.3478262E-2     au_lname, au_fname
4.3478262E-2     au_lname, au_fname, au_id
(3 row(s) affected)

Steps
--------------
Bennet
Blotchet-Halls
Carson
DeFrance
del Castillo
Dull
Green
Greene
Gringlesby
Hunter
Karsen
Locksley
MacFeather
McBadden
O'Leary
Panteley
Ringer
Ringer
Smith
Straight
```

```
Stringer
White
Yokomoto
(23 row(s) affected)
DBCC execution completed. If DBCC printed error messages, contact your
system administrator.
```

The following set of columns and their descriptions reflect output from the DBCC STATISTICS command.

Column Name	Description
Updated	Date and time the statistics were last updated
Rows	Number of rows in the table
Rows Sampled	Number of rows sampled for statistics information
Steps	Number of distribution steps
Density	Selectivity of the index
Average key length	Average length of a row
All density	Selectivity of the specified column prefix in the index
Columns	Name of the index column prefix for which All density is displayed
Steps	Number of histogram values in the current distribution statistics for the specified target on the specified table

Chapter 12

Index Maintenance

Indexes are storage structures that are used to improve performance for your queries. You can think of an index as the table of contents of a book. It doesn't tell you where each word is, but it assists you in narrowing down where you look.

As you add rows of data, remove rows of data, or update (and correspondingly move) data, the indexes no longer point at the data properly, forcing the computer to search the data without using them. This would be like having to look through an entire book to find which section you want to read. The solution to this problem used to be to drop and rebuild the indexes. With the current release of SQL Server, instead, we will simply run the DBCC REINDEX command.

Rebuilding Your Indexes

Of all the maintenance tasks that are performed worldwide on Microsoft SQL Server, index maintenance is the most neglected. This is because the amount of work to maintain them used to be excessive, the rewards for maintaining them properly are seemingly intangible, and the penalties for not maintaining them are not especially severe unless you have a high-transaction volume system. The consequence of not rebuilding your indexes, one way or another (DBCC DBREINDEX is recommended), is simply data fragmentation (which wastes space and slows down index access).

If your database is under 100 MB, you may simply not notice any effects of failure to rebuild your indexes, but maintaining the indexes periodically is still a good idea. How often do you want to do this? This depends on the size and volatility of your system. If you have a system under 1 gigabyte in size, and your volatility is below a transaction per second, monthly is probably fine. If your volume is higher, consider rebuilding more often.

DBCC DBREINDEX

This command rebuilds one or more indexes for a table in the specified database. We recommend you rebuild all indexes for each table each time. This makes it more difficult to forget one.

Syntax

```
DBCC DBREINDEX
( [ 'database.owner.table_name' [, index_name [, fillfactor ] ] ]
) [WITH NO_INFOMSGS]
```

Arguments

'database.owner.table_name'
: Name of the table for which you want to rebuild the index. If you are within the database, you can specify the name of the table only.

index_name
: This is the name of the index to rebuild. Again, we suggest you simply skip this parameter and do all indexes for the table.

fillfactor
: The percentage of space on each index page to be used for storing data when the index is created. Fillfactor replaces the original fillfactor, which was specified when the index was created, as the new default for the index and for any other non-clustered indexes that are rebuilt because a clustered index is rebuilt. When fillfactor is 0, DBCC DBREINDEX uses the original fillfactor.

WITH NO_INFOMSGS
: This option suppresses all informational messages (that is, those with severity levels from 0 through 10).

The DBCC DBREINDEX command rebuilds an index for a table or all indexes defined for a table. Since they are rebuilt dynamically, any indexes that are built to enforce either PRIMARY KEY or UNIQUE constraints can be rebuilt without having to drop and re-create those constraints. This saves you from having to find or build the data definition language (DDL) statements that are usually used to drop and then re-create the indexes.

A usage note: If you specify either index_name or fillfactor, you must specify all of the preceding parameters.

Also, the DBCC DBREINDEX command is not supported on system tables.

Output from DBCC DBREINDEX returns a result set that looks something like this unless NO_INFOMSGS is selected:

```
Index (ID = 1) is being rebuilt.
Index (ID = 2) is being rebuilt.
DBCC execution completed. If DBCC printed error messages, contact your
system administrator.
```

DBCC DBREINDEX returns this result set if the NO_INFOMSGS option is specified:

```
DBCC execution
completed. If DBCC
printed error
messages, contact
your system
administrator.
```

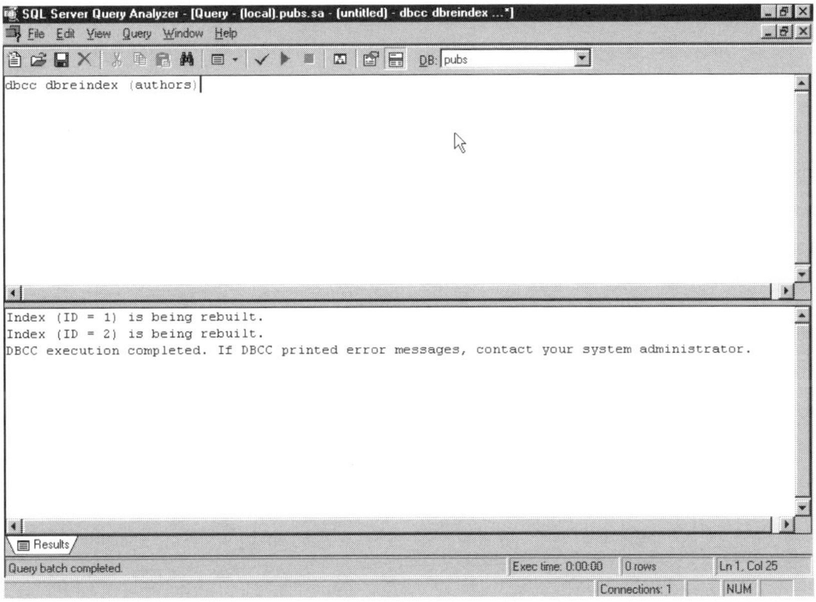

DBCC DBREINDEX is executed using the Query Analyzer program.

Chapter 13

Alerts, Operators, and Jobs

There's an old saying that goes "a watched pot never boils." It would be nice to say that "a watched server never fails," but that is usually not the case. Often times, the watched server never fails until you turn away for a second to look at something else. This leaves the poor administrator with a dilemma: stay and watch the server 24 hours a day, seven days a week, 365 days a year, or get someone or something else to do it and maintain some semblance of a life.

There are often many tasks that must be performed regularly in order for a database to run smoothly. There can often be enough tasks and conditions that an administrator must look for that little time can be left for anything else. So, to ease the burden on the administrator, SQL Server has procedures and tools to automate most of the common administrative tasks.

SQL Server Agent

These administration tasks are handled by the SQL Server Agent. This program acts as an administration assistant. The Agent scans the NT Application log and looks for the errors the administrator specifies. If any of the errors are found, the SQL Server Agent can e-mail or page an appropriate operator. If a job has been specified in response to a particular error, the job will be executed. In order for alerts, operators, and jobs to function, the SQL Server Agent must be running and have been started with an account that has the proper permissions and settings.

To start the SQL Server Agent:

1. Click the **Start** button.
2. Choose **Programs|Microsoft SQL Server 7.0|Service Manager**.
3. Choose **SQLServerAgent** from the Services box.
4. Click the **Start/Continue** button.

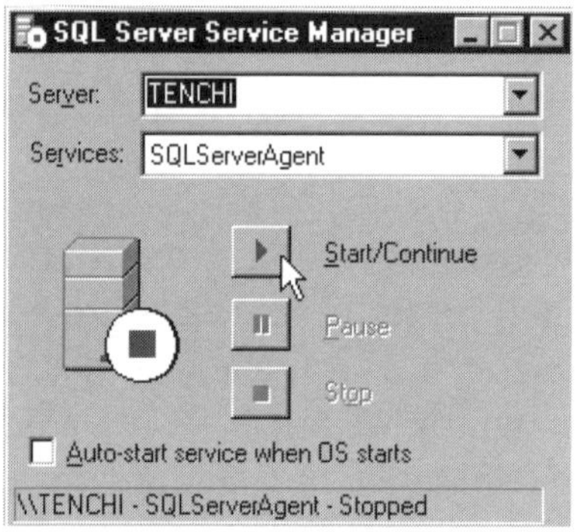

Also, in order for mail and paging to function with the SQL Server Agent, it must be configured.

To configure the SQL Server Agent to work with Windows messaging:

1. In Enterprise Manager, open the **Management** folder.
2. Right-click **SQL Server Agent**.
3. Select **Windows Messaging Settings** from the Mail profile list box.

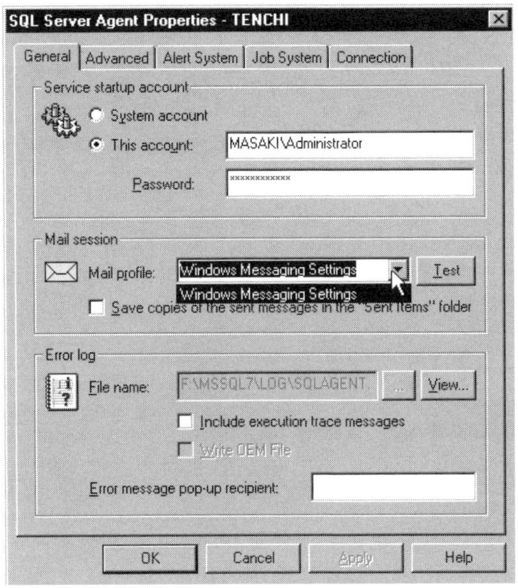

4. Click the **Test** button to test the messaging settings.
5. Click **OK** when finished.

Creating New Alerts

In order for the SQL Server Agent to perform its job, it must be told several things. The Agent must be told what to look for, what tasks to perform, and who to notify. These are the alerts, jobs, and operators. Alerts are alarms; they are what the Agent should be looking for. If any specified events happen, it will notify the appropriate people.

To create a new alert:

1. In Enterprise Manager, open the **Management** folder.
2. Open the **SQL Server Agent** item.
3. Right-click **Alerts**.
4. Click on **New Alert**.

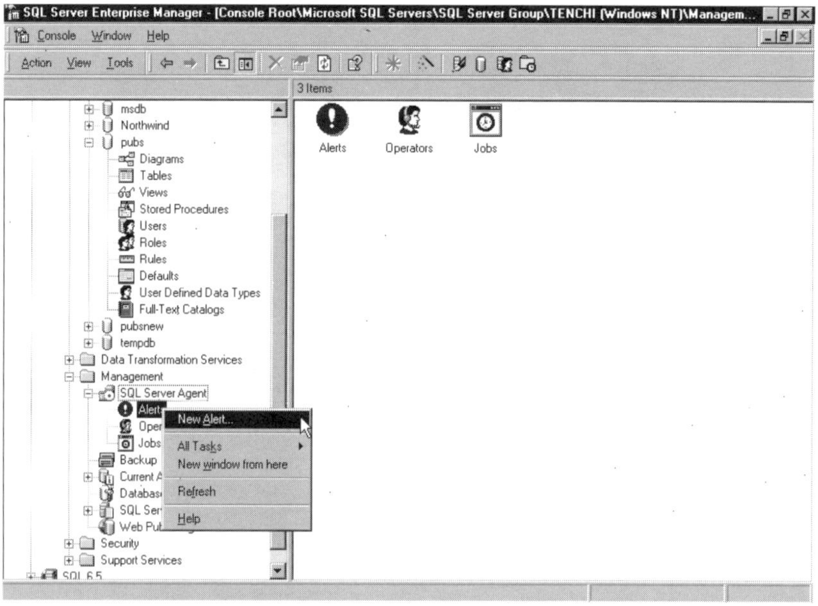

5. Enter the name of the new alert in the dialog box that appears.
6. Choose the type of alert from the Type drop-down box.
7. Choose **Error number** or **Severity**. Error number allows alerts to be defined for a specific error number. Severity allows SQL Server to define alerts based on the type of error, or its severity. For this example, the selection is Error number.

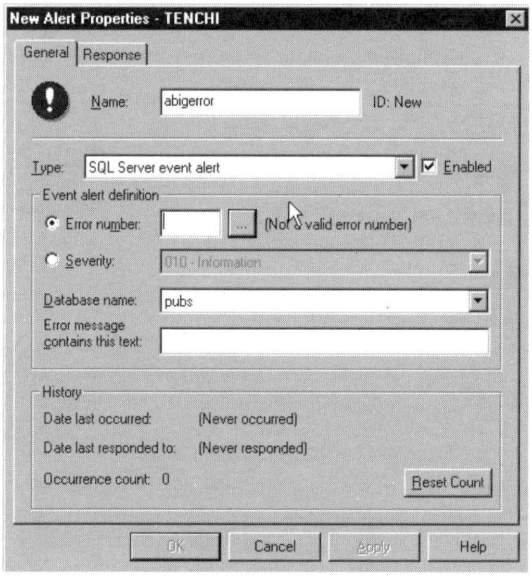

8. To locate a particular error click on the button with the ellipsis next to Error number. This will provide a search screen to locate a specific error. Type a search phrase in the Message text contains box and click the **Find** button.

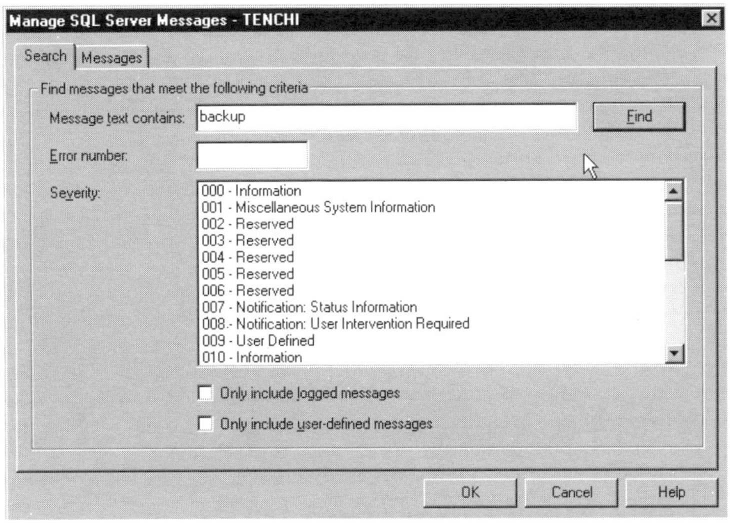

A list of related messages will be provided.

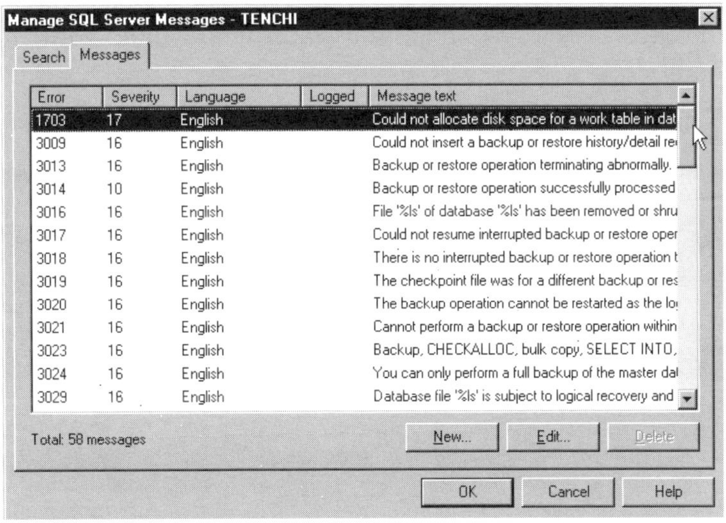

9. Note the error number, and click on the **Search** tab. Enter the error number into the appropriate box and click **OK**.

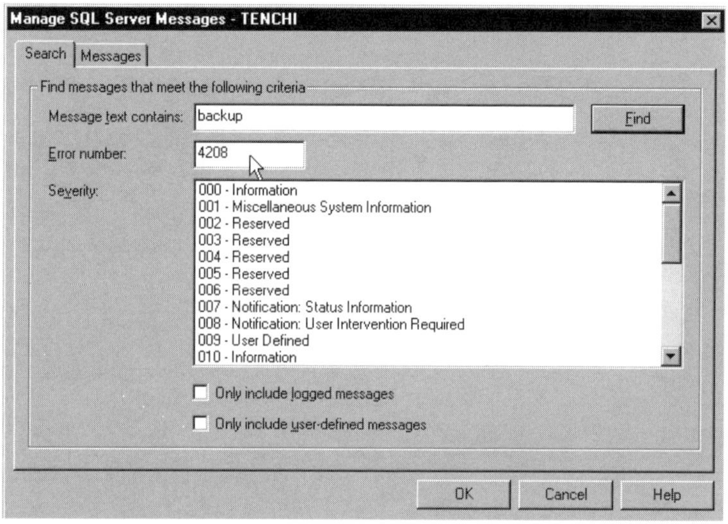

Creating New Operators

Now that the alerts have been defined, the next step is to decide who needs to know when the alert happens. These people are the operators. An operator is a system administrator who will be notified if an error is found.

To create a new operator:

1. In Enterprise Manager, open the **Management** folder.
2. Open the **SQL Server Agent**.
3. Right-click **Operators**.
4. Click **New Operator**.

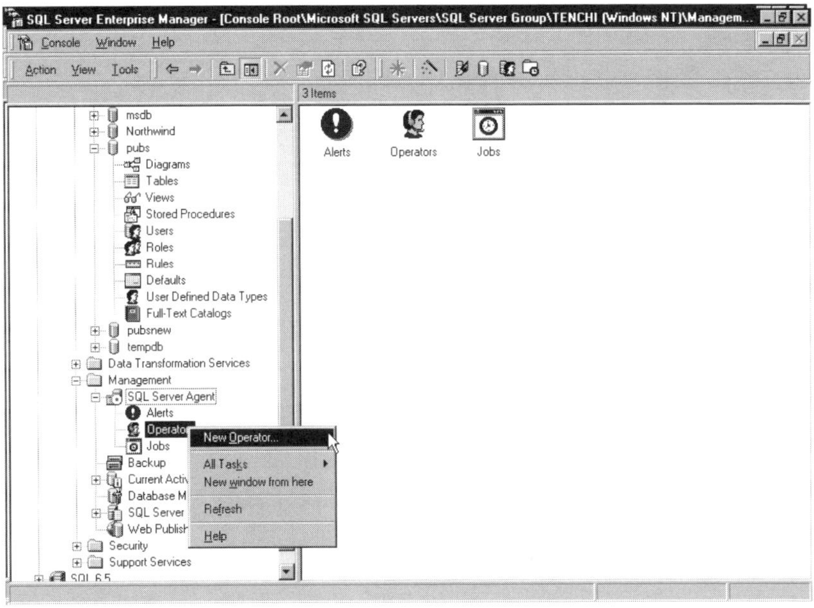

5. Type the name of the operator in the Name box.
6. Enter the e-mail address of the operator in the Email name box.
7. Enter the pager e-mail name in Pager e-mail name box.
8. Enter the net send address in the Net send address box.

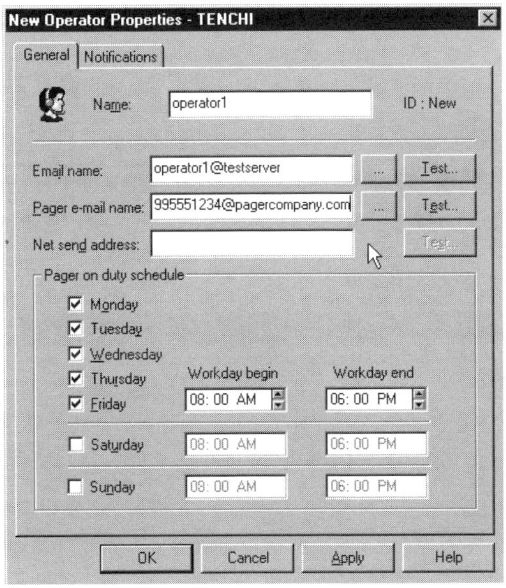

To define the notifications this operator should receive:

1. Click the **Notifications** tab.
2. Check the necessary notifications for this operator.
3. Click **OK**.

Creating New Jobs

A job is a task that the SQL Server should automatically perform. There are three kinds of jobs that the SQL Server Agent can perform.

- A Transact-SQL command (SQL statements or programs)
- An operating system command (command prompt command)
- An ActiveX Script (a program written in VBScript or JavaScript)

To set up a job:

1. In Enterprise Manager, open the **Management** folder.
2. Open the **SQL Server Agent**.
3. Right-click **Jobs**.
4. Select **New Job**.
5. Type a name for the job in the Name box of the Properties dialog.
6. Type a description for the job in the Description box.
7. Select a category for the job from the category box. Jobs can be Transact-SQL commands, but they may also be operating system commands or ActiveX programs.

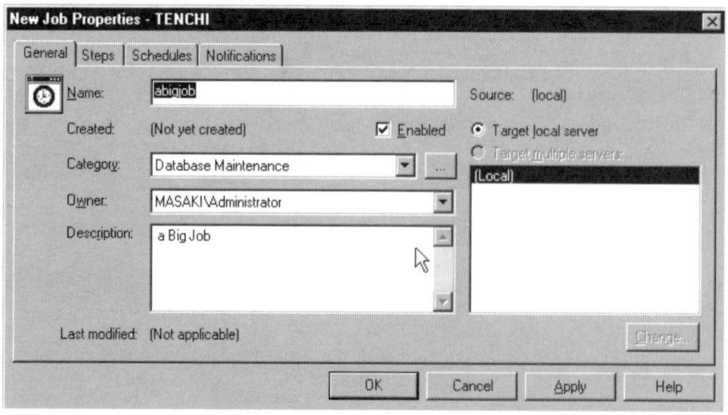

8. Click the **Steps** tab.
9. Click **New**.
10. Enter a name for the step.
11. Select the type of step (for the example, Transact-SQL).
12. Select the database involved.
13. Enter the Transact-SQL command or script to be executed.
14. Click **OK**.

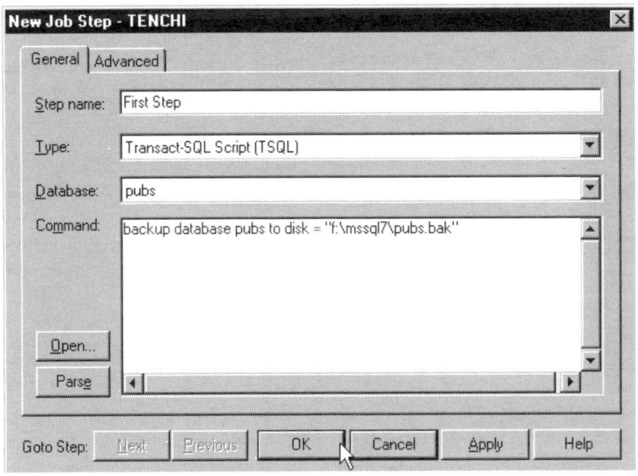

To determine a run schedule for the job:

1. Select the **Schedules** tab in the Properties dialog.
2. Select the appropriate job.
3. Click **New Schedule**.

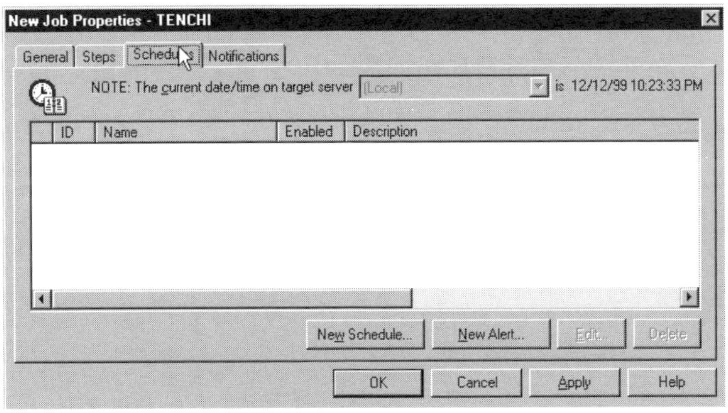

4. Decide when this task will run and select one of the following options:

Start automatically when SQL Server Agent starts
This option is self-explanatory.

Start whenever the CPU(s)become idle
This option means the task will run when the CPU is not busy with other tasks.

One time
When this is selected, a valid date and time must provided.

Recurring
This is for a repeating scheduled task.

For the example, Recurring is selected.

To alter the schedule, click the **Change** button.

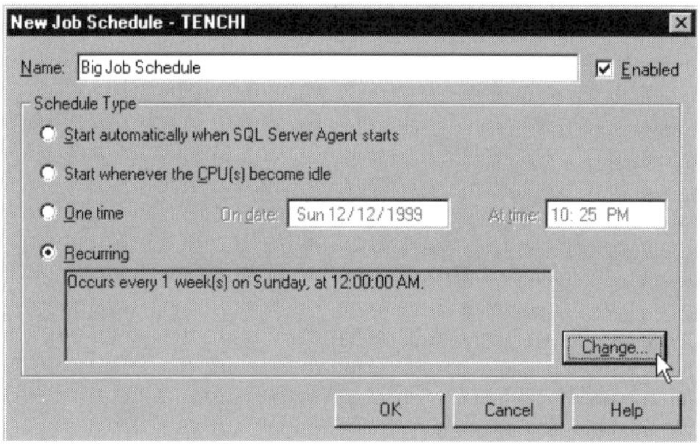

5. Select whether it is a daily, monthly, or weekly task (the example is weekly). Select any days the job should be executed. Select the time for the job to be performed in the Daily frequency section.

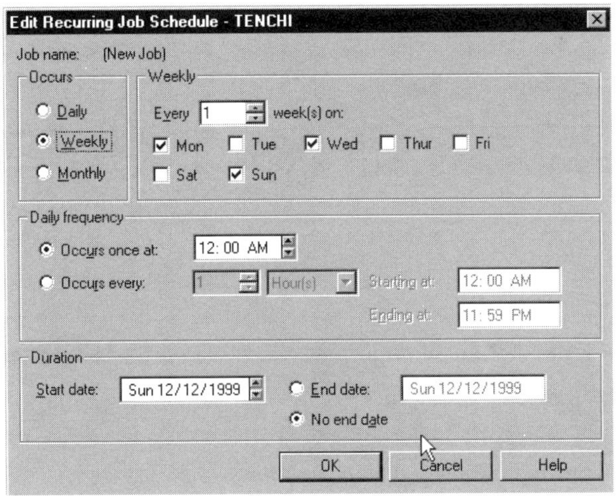

6. Click **OK**.

If any operators need to be notified of the job, click on the Notifications tab. Check off the appropriate types of notification from the different types—E-mail, Pager, or Net Send. Select the appropriate operator from the drop lists. Select when the operator should be notified of the job's conditions.

The choices are:

- When the job succeeds
- When the job fails
- Whenever the job completes

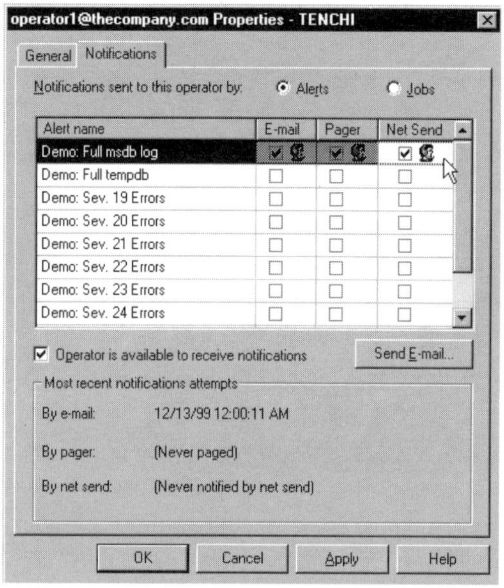

With these automation tools, the SQL Server Agent will be able to know what errors or conditions are critical to the server. The Agent will be able to notify the appropriate administrators when these errors occur and the Agent will be able to perform specific maintenance tasks on its own. This will allow the administrator to spend more time dealing with other issues rather than the day-to-day operations of the server.

Appendix A

Some Rules to Work By

Know how to get in touch with Microsoft Support. Have the appropriate telephone numbers and be prepared to pay to get your system back if it is mission critical. Do not rely on a purchased package for all of your backups; perform some normal backups as well. Think of this as insurance. It is not lucky to have coverage; it is lucky never having to file a claim. If there is a problem, run a complete system backup at that point so you can at least get back to where you are. Do this before "trying things." The current situation may not be as bad as it looks, but could be made worse than it looks.

Below are some frequently asked questions and the answers given by DBAs from around the country. Special thanks to Darren Green, Tammy Moisan, John Scances, Richard Scherrer, Lara Siren, Robert White, and Andrew Wiegand.

Blocking Problems

Problem

What is blocking and how do I determine if there is blocking on my SQL Server?

Resolution

Blocking occurs when two users are attempting to access the same resource. If one user has a lock on the record, in a table and then another user attempts to access that record the second user will be blocked by the first user.

Blocking can be identified by executing the sp_who stored procedure in Query Analyzer. Another version of sp_who is sp_who2, which returns some extra information in a format that is more readable than sp_who.

Once you have executed sp_who2, examine the BlkBy column. If you see any numbers in that column, then there is blocking on your server. Each number in the column represents a user that is blocking another user.

If you need the blocking resolved immediately, you can execute the kill command to kill the user's process (i.e., kill <number>, where <number> is the number in the BlkBy column.) Also, you can open SQL Profiler and attempt to determine the SQL being executed by the blocking user. You want to trace the SQL:Stmt:Completed event (located in the TSQL group) and filter on spid, where spid equals the number in the BlkBy column.

Blocking Process/Timeout

Problem

We have provided an Access front end to a SQL back end. We have installed the most current ODBC drivers on all computers. We use a database of parts for all jobs. Each employee is responsible for specific jobs in the database. There are one or two employees who are concerned with all jobs. When an employee opens up a query for a specific job and then another employee opens a query for all jobs and one tries to update, everyone is locked out. The following error occurs to all users:

```
ODBC - update on a linked table "Table name" failed. [Microsoft][ODBC
SQL Server Driver] Timeout expired(#0).
```

I have done lots of reading on locks, blocks, and deadlocks and I am getting the impression that SQL Server 7.0 determines the locking setup and that I should not intervene.

Resolution

What you are probably experiencing is not a SQL issue but an Access issue. There are two places to set a timeout in Access, one is global and the other is per query. More than likely your per query timeout needs to be extended.

Indexing

Problem

I received this error message when trying to reindex all indexes in a database:

```
DESCRIPTION: 17052 Table Corrupt:
Object ID 0, index ID 0, page ID (1:1172119).
The PageId in the page header = (0:0).
```

The error message repeats with different page IDs. I am unable to identify the offending table or index in the sysobjects or sysindex tables with "Object ID of 0" or "Index ID 0."

Resolution

This is most likely a transient error caused by activity in the database. Try to run DBCC in single-user mode to be sure. There is no object with an ID of 0; that's why I believe this to be a bogus error. Index ID 0, however, is your data (Index ID 1 if there is a clustered index present).

Indexing/6.5 to 7.0 Upgrade

Problem

I've just upgraded my database from SQL Server 6.5 to SQL Server 7.0 and I notice there are many new indexes that did not exist in my 6.5 database. All of these new indexes start with "_WA". Where did they come from?

Resolution

These are not really indexes but statistics on data distribution for columns in your tables. SQL Server uses these statistics to determine the best execution plan for queries. By default, SQL Server will automatically create statistics on your columns. You can determine if SQL Server is automatically creating statistics with the following SQL:

```
sp_dboption <database name>
```

Do you see an option called "auto create statistics"? If so, SQL Server is automatically creating statistics. In general, this is a good thing and you should leave this option turned on.

Overallocated Memory

Problem

I have overallocated memory for SQL Server and now it will not start. What can I do?

Resolution

To recover from this:

1. Stop SQL Server and SQL Executive. Also make sure that SQL Enterprise Manager isn't running.
2. Go to the <sql>\binn directory and type **sqlservr -c –f**. This will start SQL in single-user mode with a minimum config.
3. Ignore the text messages in this window—but wait for them to finish appearing (shouldn't take more than 10-20 seconds). SQL Server is now started.
4. Go to another window and start ISQL/W and connect locally with the SA userid.
5. In ISQL/W issue the following commands :

```
sp_configure memory, <new memory value>
go
reconfigure
go
```

6. Now go back to the window SQL is running in; type **shutdown** and press **enter**.
7. SQL Server should shut down. If it doesn't, press **Ctrl+C** to shut it down.
8. Now you should be able to start SQL normally and connect.

Installing SQL Server

Problem

I'm having trouble installing SQL Server. What could be going wrong?

Resolution

Try the following checklist of things that could go wrong. I have never known anyone not to install SQL after following these instructions. (If you're the first, then let me know.)

1. Make sure you have administrator level permissions on the machine in question, as SQL needs to create registry entries, services, etc.
2. Make sure the machine is of the required spec to run the version of SQL you are installing (i.e., if it is SQL EE then make sure you have NT EE. For SQL 7.0 you need a 100% PENTIUM compatible chip or an Alpha).

If you have tried to install SQL before, then manually clean up all the files/registry entries as follows:

- Remove the <sql> directory and everything under it
- Remove the <sql> dir from the path (use Control Panel|System for this)
- Remove the SQL registry entries using regedt32|regedit. These are:

(All versions)

- HKEY_LOCAL_MACHINE\SYSTEM\CurrentControlSet\Services\MSSQLServer
- HKEY_LOCAL_MACHINE\SOFTWARE\Microsoft\MSSQLServer

(6.0 and above)

- HKEY_LOCAL_MACHINE\System\CurrentControlSet\Services\MSDTC
- HKEY_LOCAL_MACHINE\SYSTEM\CurrentControlSet\Services\SQLExecutive

(7.0 and above)

- HKEY_LOCAL_MACHINE\SYSTEM\CurrentControlSet\Services\SQLServerAgent
- HKEY_LOCAL_MACHINE\Software\Microsoft\Microsoft SQL Server 7
- HKEY_LOCAL_MACHINE\Software\Microsoft\MSSQLServ65

If you have lost permission to any of the registry keys, then log on as administrator and take ownership of them starting at the highest relevant level. Use regedt32 and check the box to take ownership of all subkeys as well.

If SQL is complaining about not enough space being there, this could be due to a known bug when there is between <n> times 4,295,917 KB and <n> times 4,367,417 KB. To get around this, either create temporary files to use space up, or start the SQL setup program as follows. Spacing is important.

```
<sqldir>\i386\setup /t SpaceChecking = Off
```

SQL Server is dependent on network functionality—even for the setup routines. Specifically it needs to use named-pipe/mailslot functionality (on NT machines—see number 6 for Win9x). These usually require a network card to be present. If you don't have a network card, then go to Control Panel|Networks, choose Add Adapter and then add the Microsoft loopback adapter—which is just a dummy driver, no hardware involved. This needs to have working network protocol(s) bound to it. Let whichever protocols you have use default parameters, <u>except</u> for TCP/IP. If you are using this then do <u>not</u> specify DHCP assigned address, use 192.168.1.1 as the IP address and 255.255.255.0 as the subnet mask. This is a standard RFC1918 non-routed IP address so it shouldn't clash with any dial-up address you may be given by an ISP. If you are using the IPX/SPX protocol, accept the default frame type of 802.3.

If the server service does not start after installing the loopback adapter and you get the message "The server service was terminated" with the following error: `"Not enough server storage is available to process this command in the event log,"` then you need to reinstall your NT service pack to synchronize your NT networking files.

SQL Server Version

Problem

How do I determine what version of SQL Server I'm using?

Resolution

Execute the following extended stored procedure in Query Analyzer and examine the ProductVersion field:

```
exec master.dbo.xp_msver
```

Transaction Log is Full

Problem

How do I recover from a full log error?

Resolution

1. Issue log backup with TRUNCATE_ONLY for database.
2. Create a table in the problem database, insert a row, and issue a few updates. I do 100 updates in a while loop; this will move the active VLF to an earlier physical location.
3. Issue DBCC SHRINKDATABASE with NOTRUNCATE to mark a shrinkpoint:

   ```
   DBCC SHRINKDATABASE( @dbName , NOTRUNCATE )
   ```

4. Issue log backup with TRUNCATE_ONLY for database to force the shrink:

```
BACKUP LOG @dbName WITH TRUNCATE_ONLY
```

5. Now issue FULL DATABASE BACKUP.

After all that, you should have a backup of your database with a pretty clean log file. The log should show up as being almost completely unused.

The following stored proc will execute all this logic, and can be run to recover from a full transaction log. It can be set up to run automatically from a performance monitor alert.

```
CREATE PROC dbo.LogFull @dbName VARCHAR(128) , @backupLoc VARCHAR(128)
AS

/**********************************************************************
**
* Stored Procedure: LogFull
*
*
* Purpose: Recovers from log full errors
*
* Input Parameters: @dbName VARCHAR(128) – pass in the name of the
* database that has a full log
* @backupDir VARCAHR(128) full path to store backup file
*
* Output Parameters: NONE
*
* Return Status: Always 0
*
* Usage: EXEC admin.dbo.LogFull 'database_name' ,
'd:\sqlbackups\dbdump.BAK'
*
* Local Variables: <list all local variables>
* @NOW DATETIME Current date/time
* @tblName VARCHAR(128) name for a temporary table created by this
procedure.
*
* Called By: to be invoked by the DBA when a log fills up
*
```

```
* Calls: NONE
*
* Data Modifications: NONE
*
* Result Set: NONE
*
* Permissions: SYSADMIN
*
*********************************************************************
*/
DECLARE @NOW DATETIME
DECLARE @tblName VARCHAR(128)

IF @dbname IN ( 'master' , 'tempdb' )
BEGIN
 RAISERROR ('CANNOT BACKUP LOG on master or tempdb' , -1 , -1 )
 RETURN 0
END
--
-- Issue log backup with TRUNCATE_ONLY for database
--
 BACKUP LOG @dbName WITH TRUNCATE_ONLY
--
-- Create a table in the problem database,
-- Insert a row,
-- Issue a few updates.
-- This will move the active VLF to an earlier physical location.
--
-- Create a table name using spid and datetime:
SELECT @tblName = 'logShrink_' + REPLACE ( REPLACE ( @dbName +
 + ' ' + CONVERT( VARCHAR(16) , @@SPID )
 + ' ' + CONVERT( VARCHAR(35) , @NOW , 113 ) , ':' , '_' ) , ' ' , '_'
)

EXEC (' use ' + @dbName
 + ' SET NOCOUNT ON CREATE TABLE ' + @tblName + ' ( col1 int )
 INSERT ' + @tblName + '(col1) VALUES(1)
 DECLARE @I INT
 SET @I = 0
 WHILE ( @I < 101 )
```

```
 BEGIN
 UPDATE ' + @tblName + ' SET col1 = @I
 SET @I = @I + 1
 END
 DROP TABLE ' + @tblName )
--
-- Issue DBCC SHRINKDATABASE to mark a shrinkpoint
--
 DBCC SHRINKDATABASE( @dbName , NOTRUNCATE )
--
-- Issue log backup with TRUNCATE_ONLY for database to move allocated
pages to front of files
--
 BACKUP LOG @dbName WITH TRUNCATE_ONLY
--
-- NOW ISSUE FULL DATABASE BACKUP:
--

 BACKUP DATABASE @dbName TO DISK = @backupLoc

GO
```

Appendix B

For Further Information

If you would like further information on SQL Server, or a place to go online to ask experts for help, here are some good places to start.

http://people.mw.mediaone.net/overthrow/index.html
http://www.soaringeagleltd.com
http://www.microsoft.com/sql/
http://www.microsoft.com/mcp/certstep/mcdbaben.htm
http://www.pinpub.com/sqlpro/home.htm
http://www.sqlpass.org/
http://www.deja.com/dnquery.xp?search=word&svcclass=dncurrent&showsort=date&ST=QS&query=~g%20comp.databases.ms-sqlserver
http://support.microsoft.com/support/sql/papers.asp
http://www.geocities.com/~dsnydersql/links/links.htm
http://www.sqlmag.com/index.html
http://www.sqlserver.com/
http://www.swynk.com/sqlhome/scriptlibrary.asp

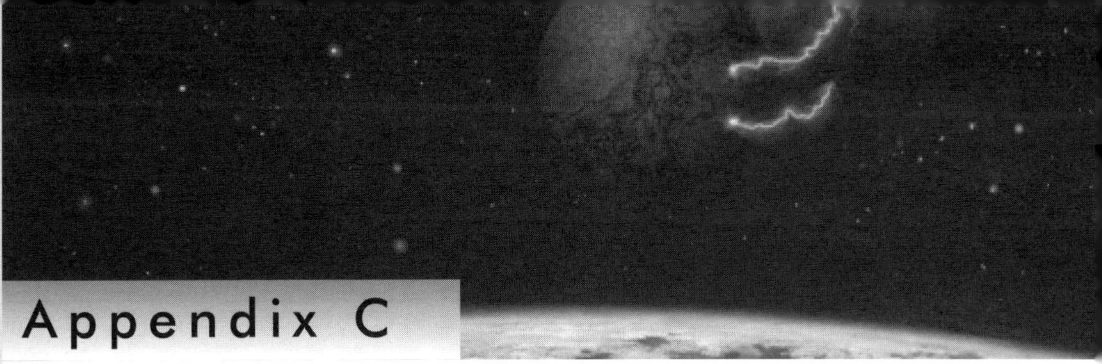

Appendix C

The Wizards

Wizard is a term used by Microsoft to describe tools that try to automatically figure out some of the tasks that might otherwise require a great deal of work, research, and/or thought. This appendix will cover the SQL Server wizards that have not already been discussed in this book. We will recommend settings and some changes that you may have to make for your particular database system.

If you get this screen when you open the Enterprise Manager, click on the Show/Hide button.

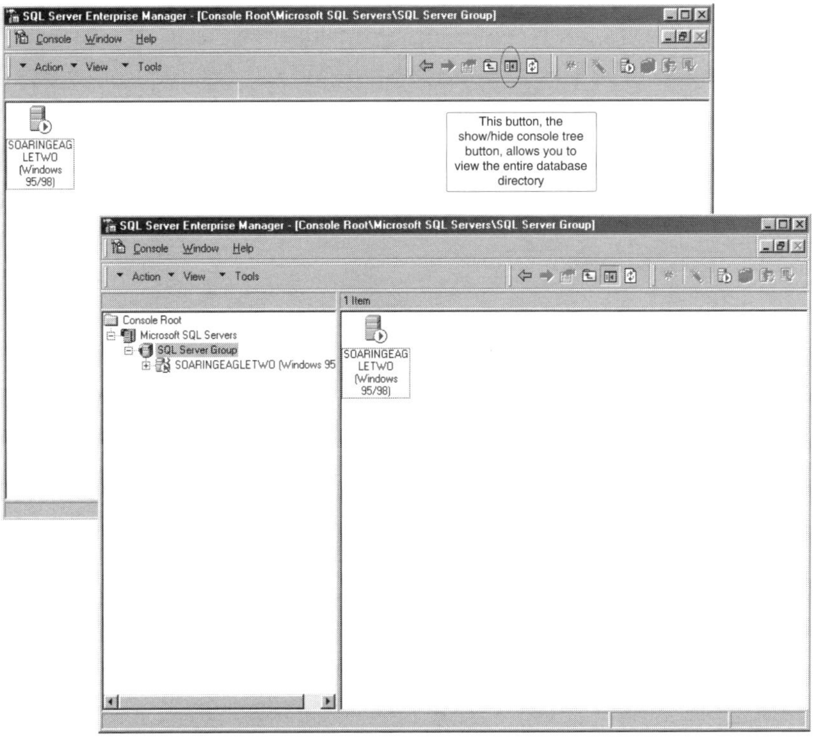

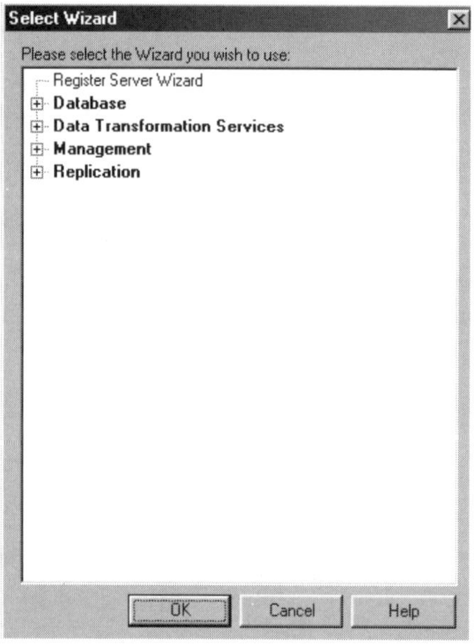

At the top of this screen you see Action, View, and Tools. Click on **Tools**. The Select Wizard window will pop up.

The Create Database Wizard

You can use the Create Database Wizard, rather than manually create database statements, to create your database initially. To use this, double-click on the **Create Database Wizard** selection (making sure that you have selected a server in the drop-down tree on the left).

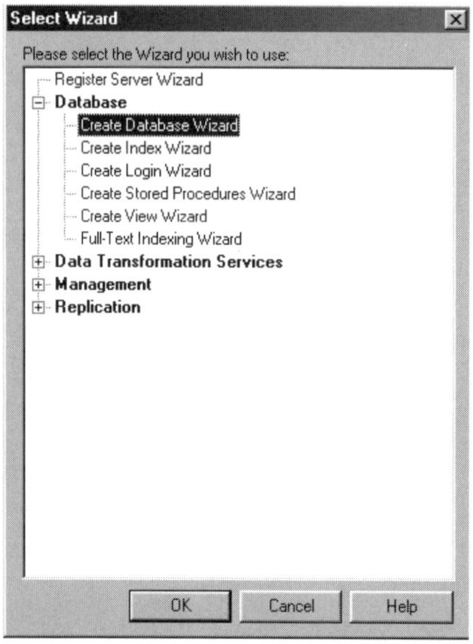

The welcome window will appear.

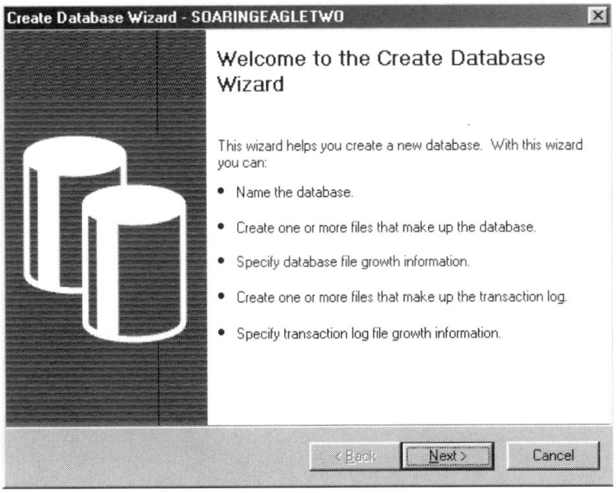

Click **Next** and the following window appears. You will have to decide upon a name for the database. We recommend less than 30 characters, and we further recommend you exclude spaces and punctuation marks. The location is the place where you want the server to preallocate space for the database. If possible, this should be a physical disk that is set aside for this purpose.

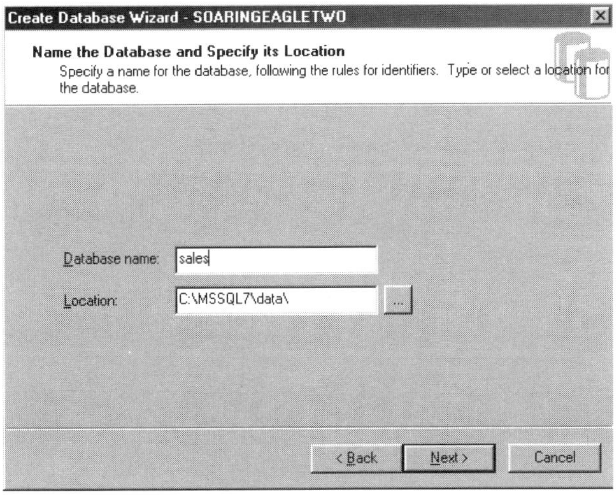

Next, name the database files on this screen:

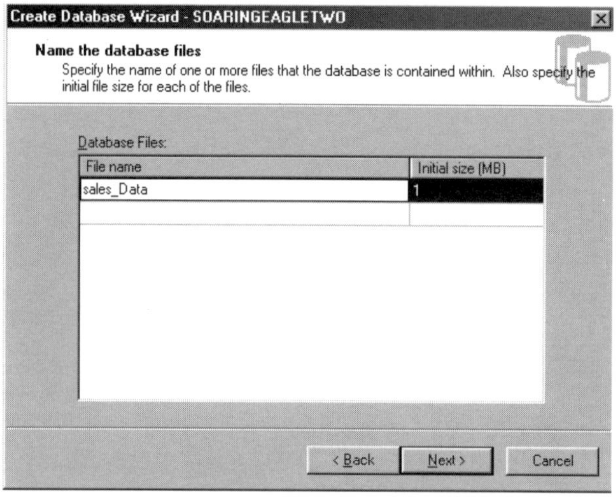

File names should correspond with normal file naming conventions for your operating system. File size is much more easily managed if you set it to automatically grow as needed. Remember, your unit of backup is the database, so if you keep it small, and only grow it as necessary, you can back up the least amount of database, while still being able to use all of the space on your disk. There is no reason not to allow the database to start small. You might consider restricting the file growth to the size of your disk.

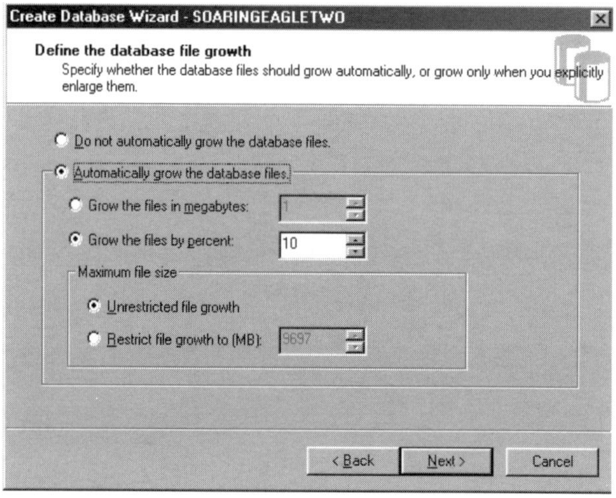

The transaction log file also meets naming conventions for your operating systems. You should name the database file and log file something similar but different, so that you know which is which, and which file(s) are for which databases.

Click **Next**. As with database file growth, transaction log file growth should be set to automatically grow as needed.

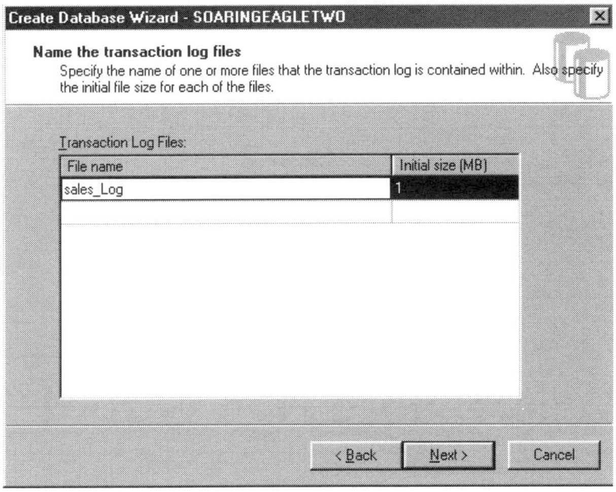

Click **Next**. To complete the creation of your database, click **Finish**.

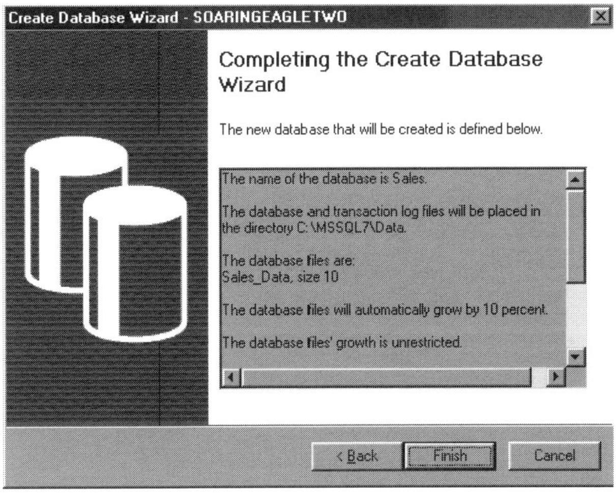

A message will appear to confirm that the database was successfully completed.

The wizard will then give you the option to create a maintenance plan for your database.

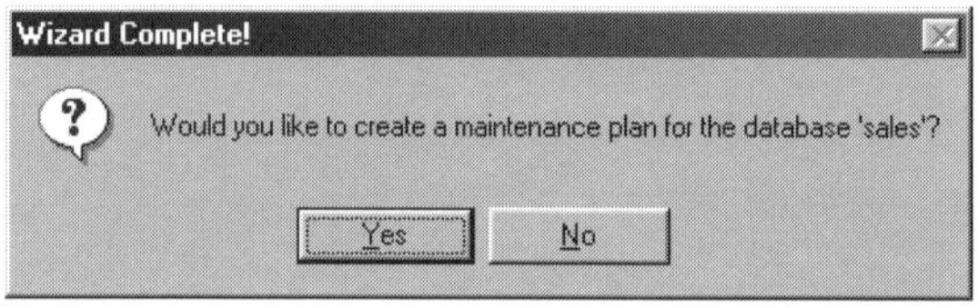

The Database Maintenance Plan Wizard

This topic was already discussed, at length, at the end of Chapter 2, but is repeated here for convenience. If you clicked Yes in the previous window, you will see the welcome screen to the Database Maintenance Plan Wizard.

Click **Next**. Here we are going to build a maintenance plan for only one database, the Sales database which we have already created. Click on **These databases** and scroll down until you find your database. Select your database and click **Next**.

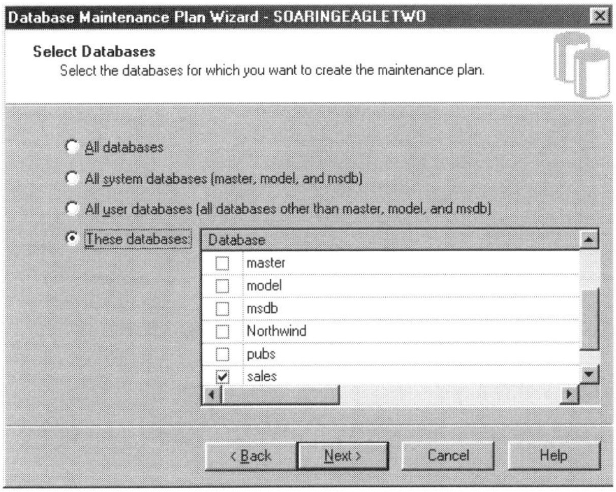

Make sure you check each of the three main check boxes. The numbers selected here are a good start, unless your database vendor has recommended alternate settings.

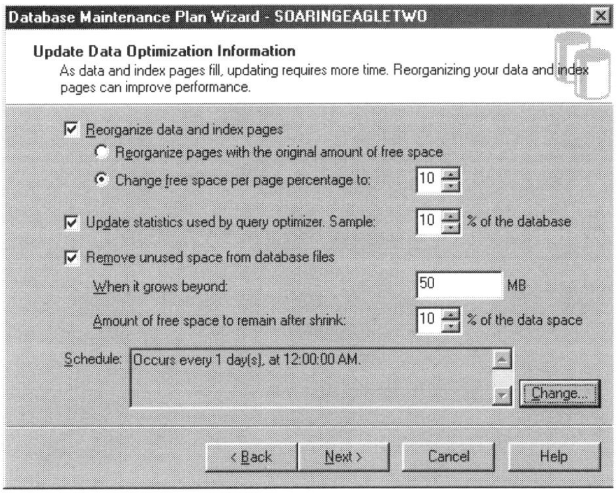

You can alter your schedule by clicking the Change button. You can create many schedules, and name them accordingly.

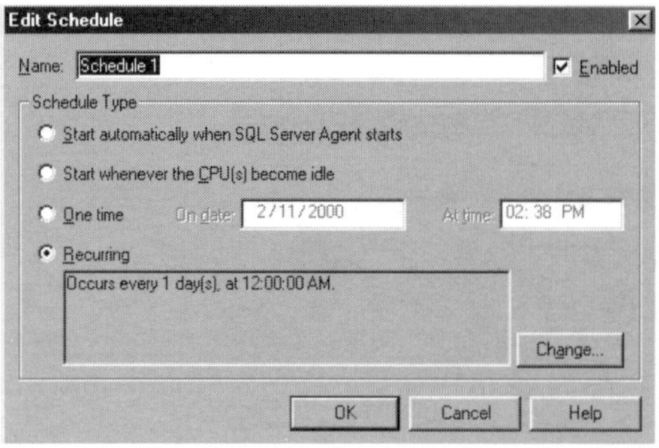

Click **OK** and **Next** to schedule database and internal data integrity tests.

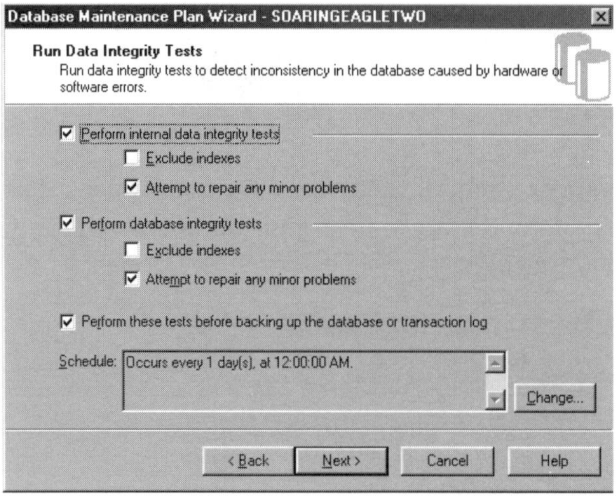

Press **Next** to finish or the **Change** button to customize a schedule.

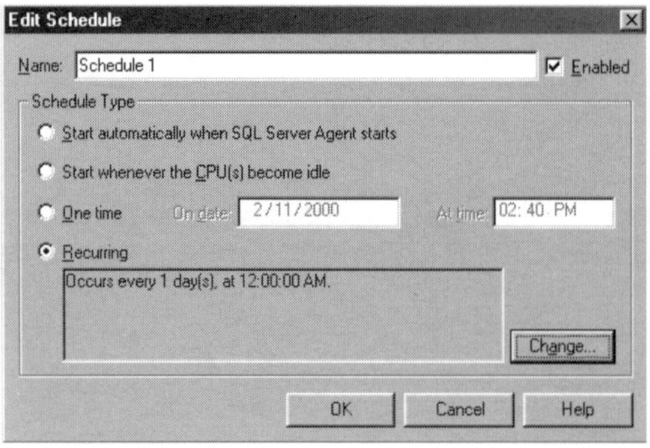

Remember this schedule window? You can schedule maintenance to be performed all at once or at different times. All of this should be scheduled when the system is not in heavy use. Press **OK** when you are finished.

Specify the Database Backup Plan

The next step in the wizard is to specify where, when, and how the backups will take place. This would be a good time to refer to your backup plan. Be sure that you are backing up to the correct device. Be sure that you are backing up often enough for your environment. Remember to check to be sure that the backups occurred. Then get the backup off-site.

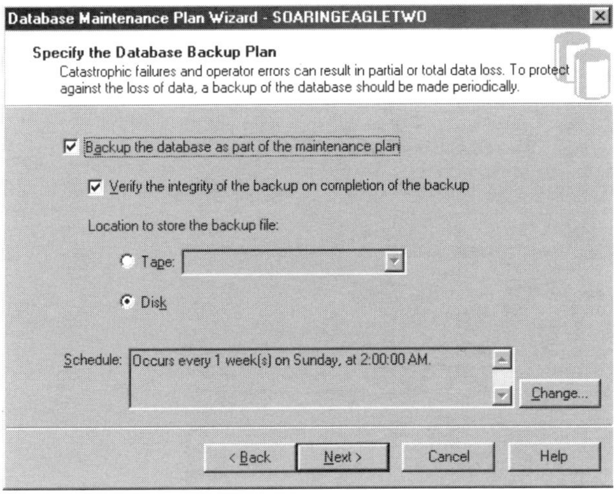

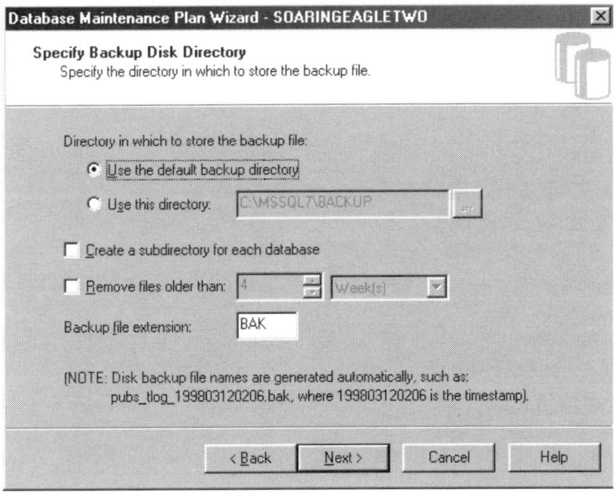

Specify the Transaction Log Backup Plan

Remember that if your transaction log fills SQL Server will pause. Therefore, the decision to back up this log is crucial. You will want to monitor the transaction log to recognize normal growth patterns, understand high-volume cycles, and determine the best time to perform backups for your database. Please refer to Chapter 8.

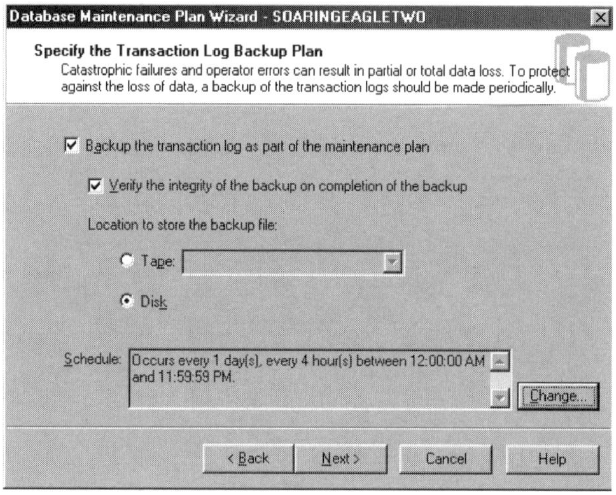

As you can see, this process is similar to specifying database backups. However, you may want to be careful with your selection for the Remove files older than option. Think about how volatile your data needs are and the space you have on your hard drive or disk(s).

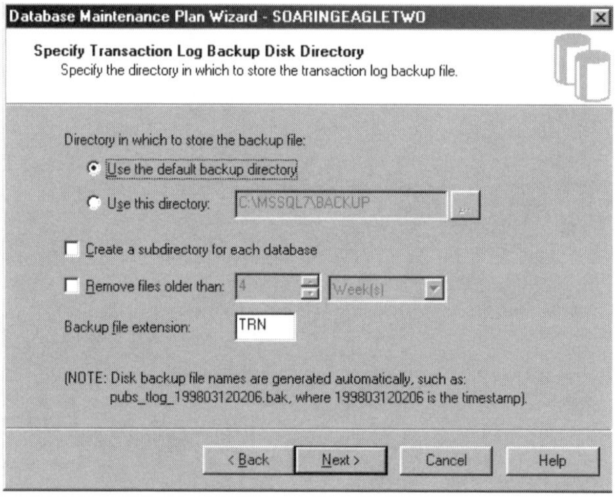

Select your reporting option in accordance with your business environment. Do not skip this step. An actual record of the maintenance plan occurring may be helpful for a multitude of tasks and problem solving issues over time.

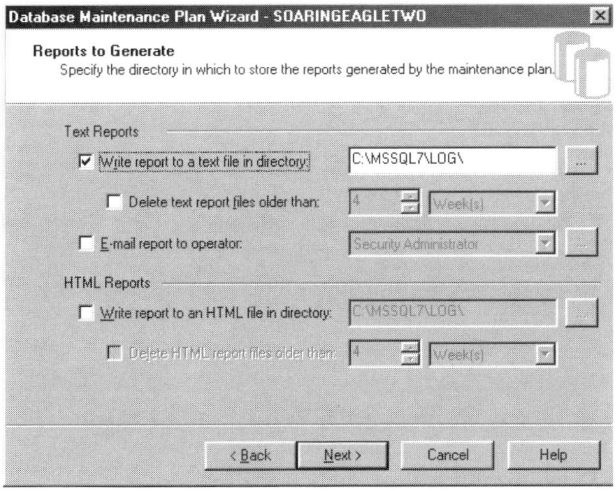

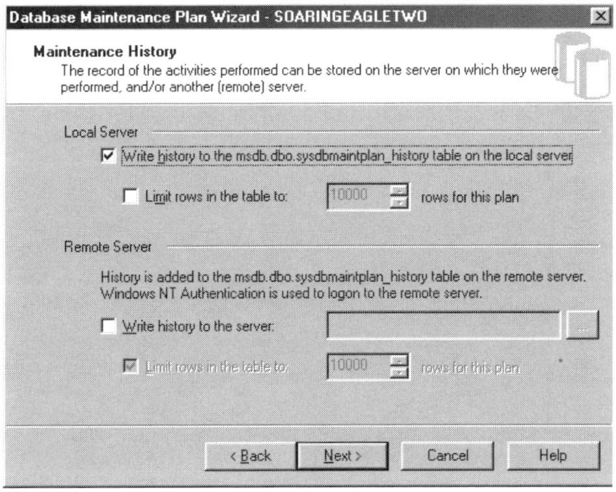

For the final step in this wizard, name your database plan to coincide with the database. Then click **Finish**.

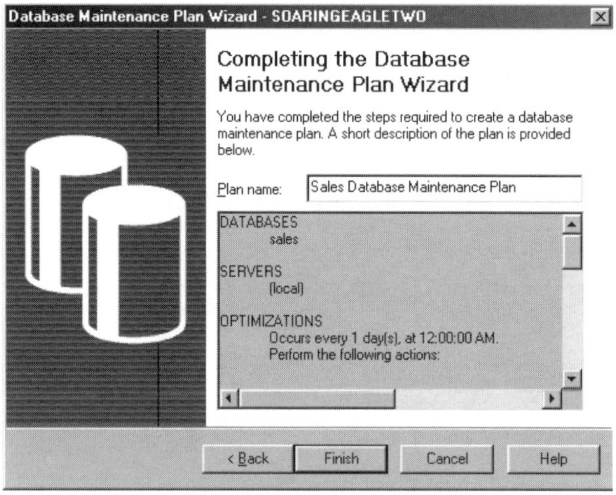

To see your newly created database maintenance plan, search down the directory, find Database Maintenance Plans, and click on it.

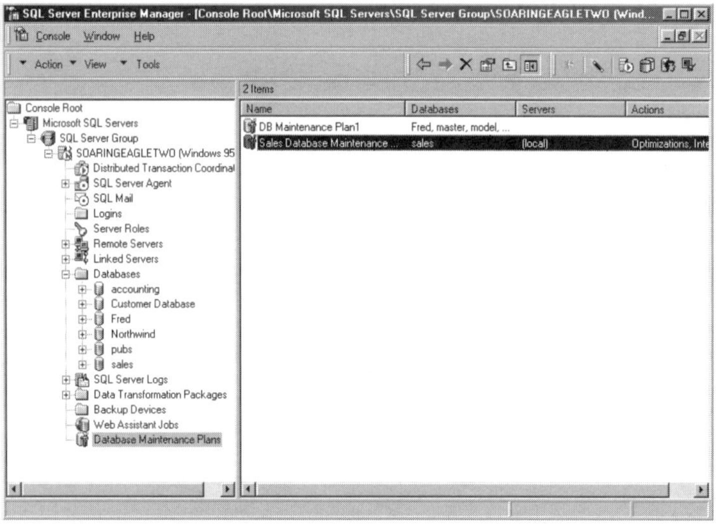

The Create Login Wizard

The Create Login Wizard helps to give users access to the SQL Server.

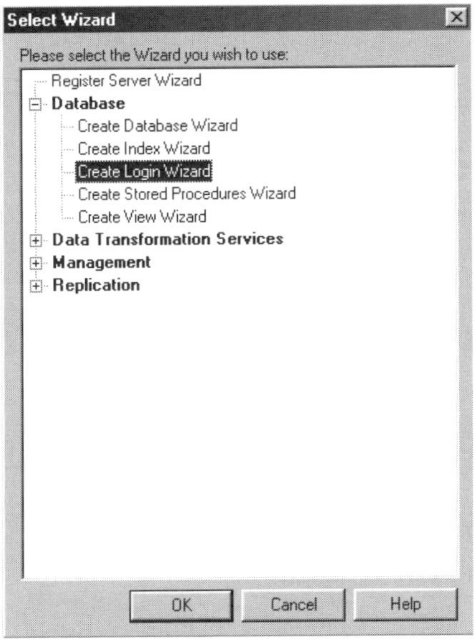

The initial wizard screen should look familiar by now:

Use the authentication recommended by your software vendor. Here, we are using SQL Server authentication, rather than NT authentication.

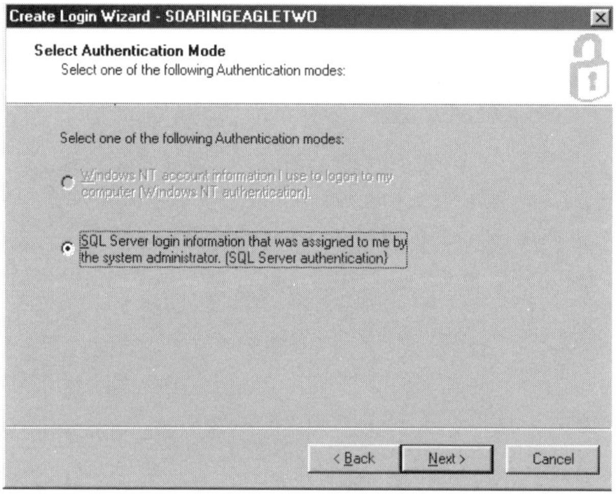

For security reasons, we recommend passwords be at least six characters, and include special characters and/or numbers.

Most of your users will not have any of the following options checked, unless special roles were created by your software vendor.

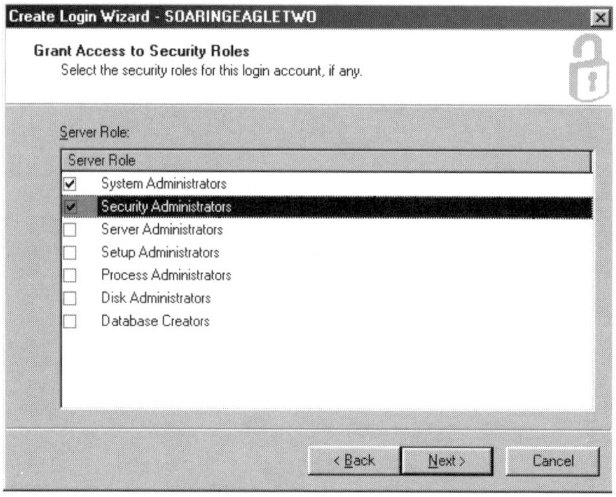

Access to the server does not guarantee access to any of the user databases. Give users access to the appropriate database.

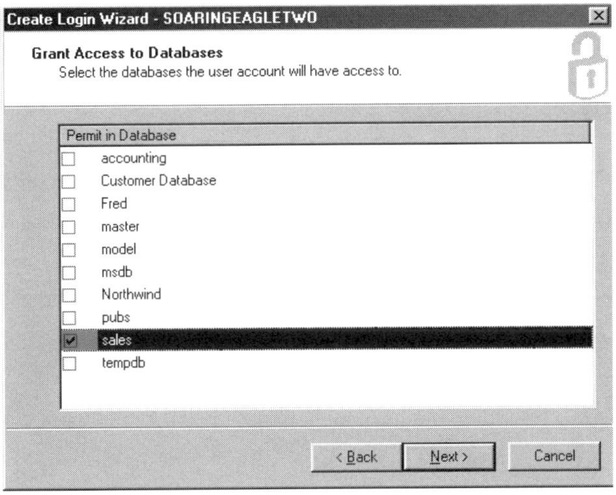

Click **Finish** to confirm your selections and complete the wizard.

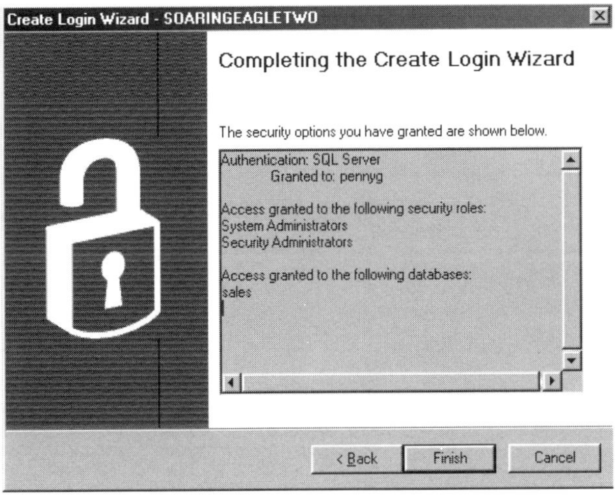

The Management Wizards

Here we'll look at a couple of the management wizards available to you.

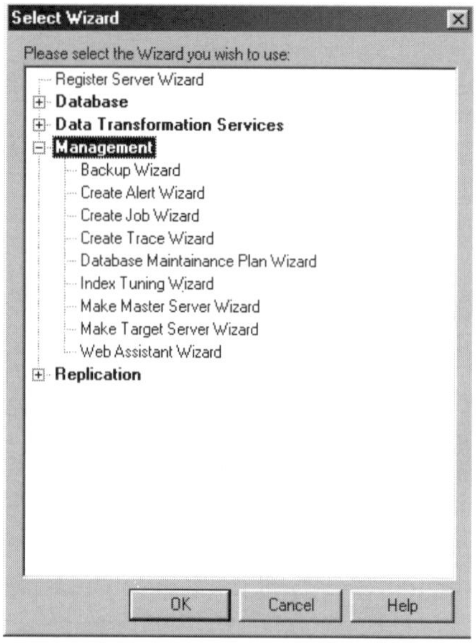

The Backup Wizard

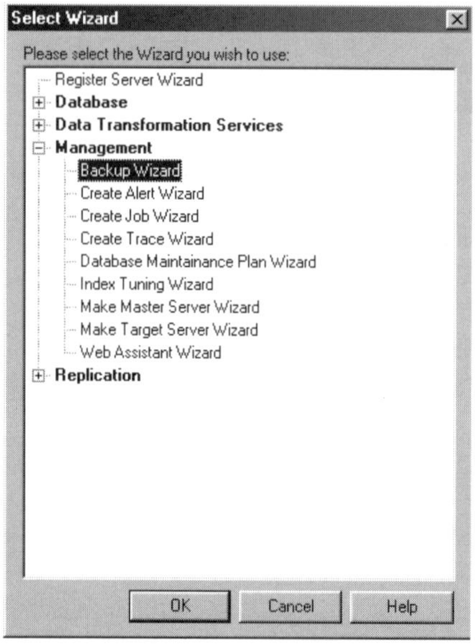

The Backup Wizard exists to help you automate the backing up of your databases to a specific device on a specific schedule.

If you double-click on Backup Wizard, you will get the familiar wizard starting screen:

Click **Next** to get to the following screen, which allows you to pick the database for which you'd like to set up a backup plan.

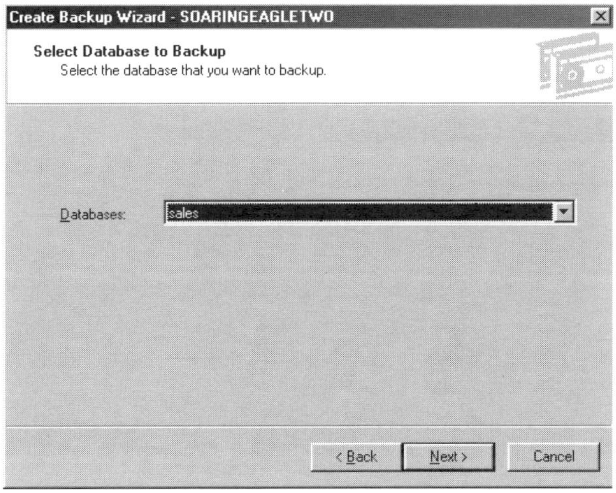

Since we have been using the Sales database that we have just created, we will continue to use this as an example. The description here is optional. If you have only one database, the description is not necessary. Click **Next**.

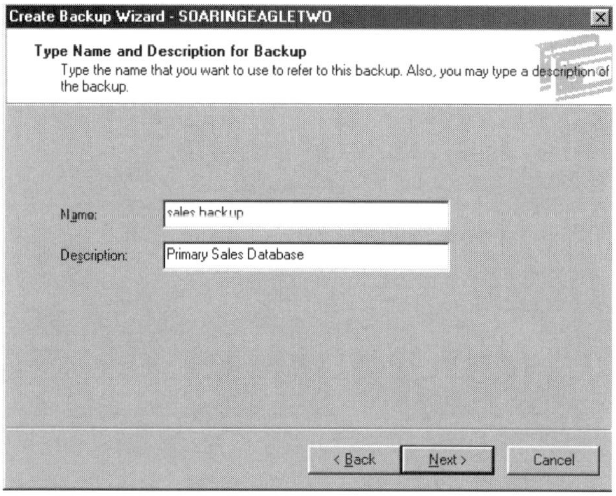

If you are going to automate your backups we suggest that you use the complete backup scenario. Ignore the differential backup and the transaction log options given to you on this screen.

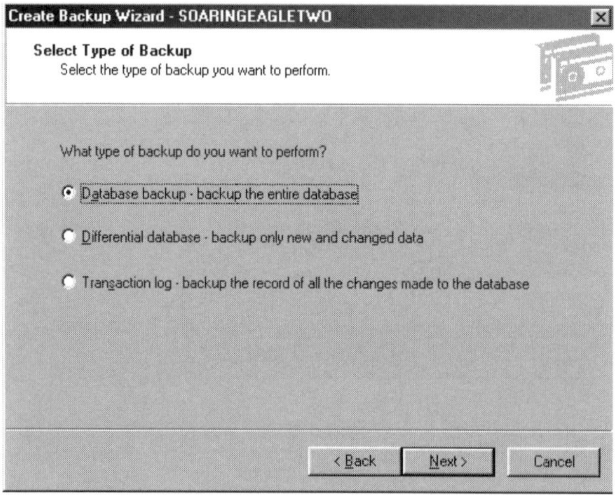

You will have to click on the Add button to define a new backup device. Also decide whether you want to append or overwrite your backup media. There are two paths to follow here. One is Append to the backup media. If, for example, you have a very large tape, and a very small database, you may want to simply collect all of the database backups on a single tape, which might sit in the tape drive until it is needed (note that this is not a substitute for getting your backups off-site). The other is to replace the contents of a backup media each time. We prefer to use fresh media each time and remove the media from the site. The next couple of screens will first follow the Append to the backup media path.

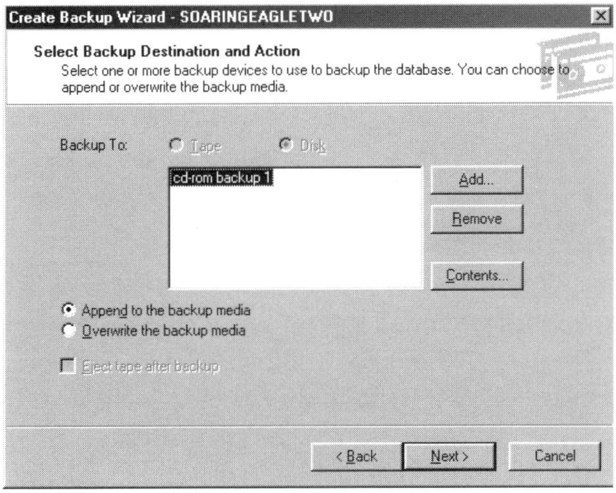

Choose your backup device, and then click **OK**.

When you choose Append, the Backup set will expire option is not active. Choose a descriptive media name and choose **Verify backup upon completion**. Both of these selections are useful tools to allow you to track problems if or when they occur.

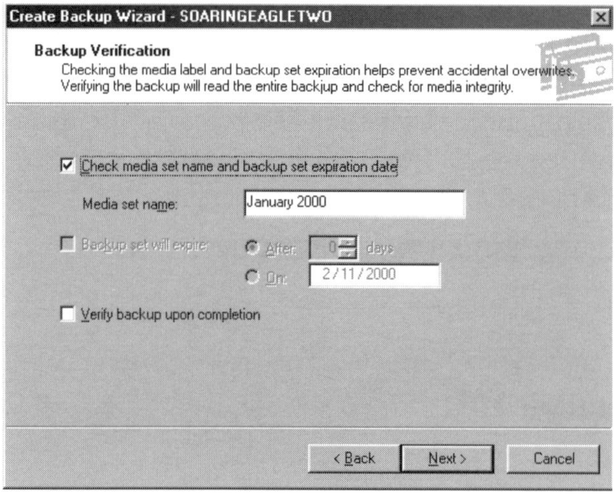

Initialize and label media will be selected as a default. Allow this to stay selected. Enter a descriptive media set name. As you are going through this naming process, follow the naming conventions that you have set up to be sure that anyone following through this process later will know exactly what to do. This will help resolve any human error issues in tracking problems and processes later.

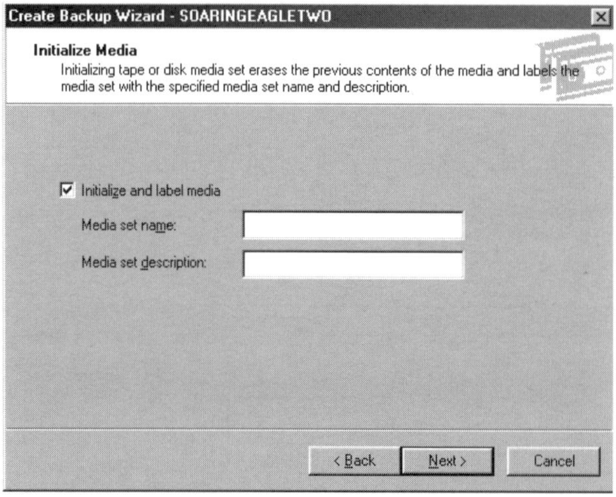

If you choose to overwrite the backup media in the Select Backup Destination and Action window, the wizard will skip directly to the Initialize Media window.

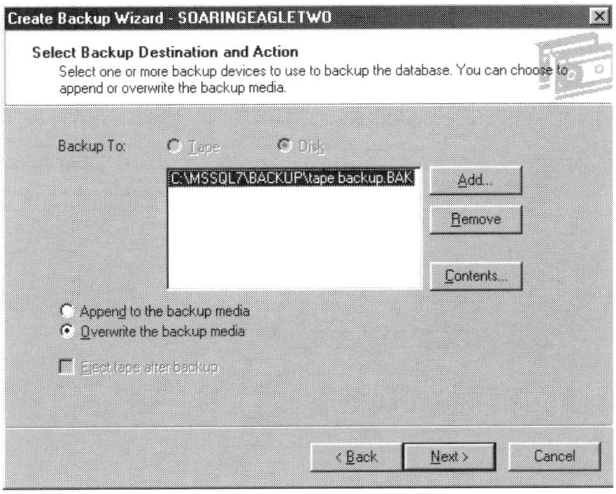

This screen asks you to choose a name to set for the tape description. Remember in Chapter 8 we discussed appropriate naming conventions and the importance of establishing them. If you have not set a naming convention when you have come to this point, stop for a couple of minutes and describe one in a document that is available to others and then stick with that convention unless a change has been documented. Be sure that it is descriptive enough to identify the tape quickly and precisely under stressful conditions.

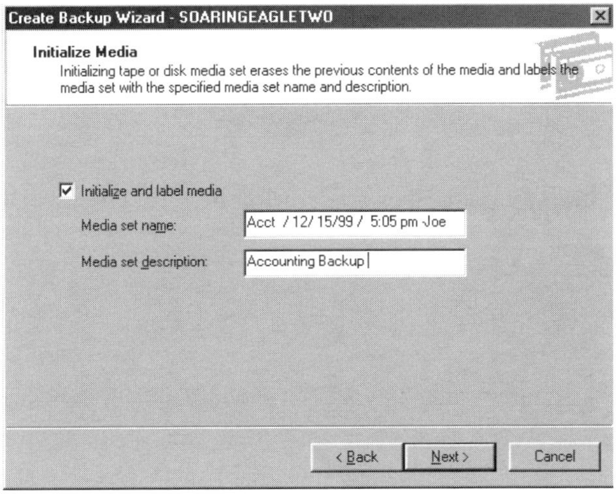

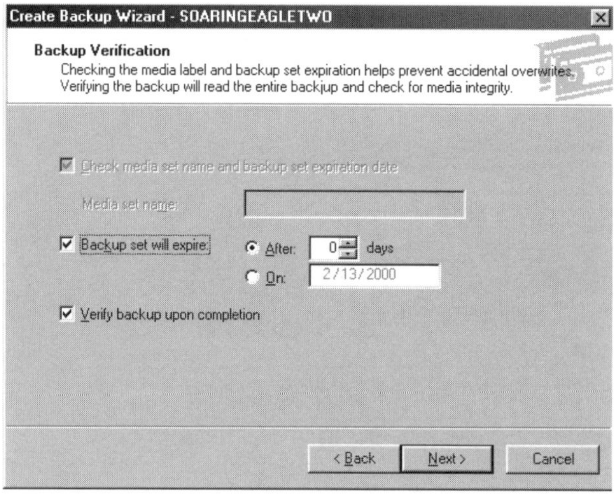

As you can see, the Backup set will expire selection now becomes active since it is relevant to this type of media backup. Consider all of the aspects of your system processes as you choose this timing selection.

Review this screen to be sure that everything seems to be correct and click on the **Finish** button.

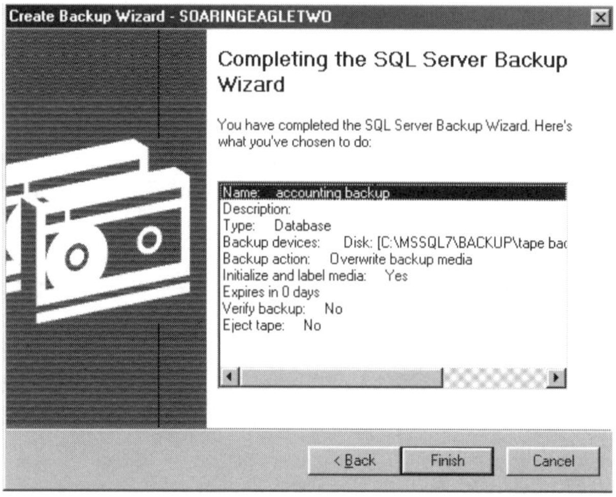

Your automated backup processes are complete.

Now remember to put the backup media in the drive, label it, and then take it off-site.

The Create Alert Wizard

Alerts, jobs, and operators are objects that are created to define automated problem solving techniques. We are going to create an example of how to set up an alert to notify you that someone has tried to enter your system without authorized access.

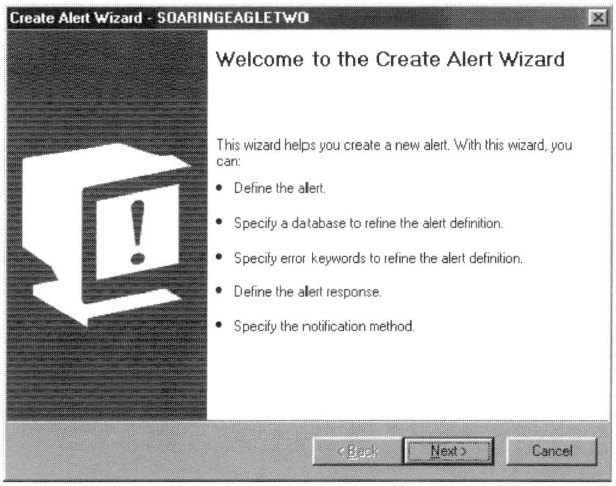

If you select the down arrow you'll see that many selections are pre-described for you.

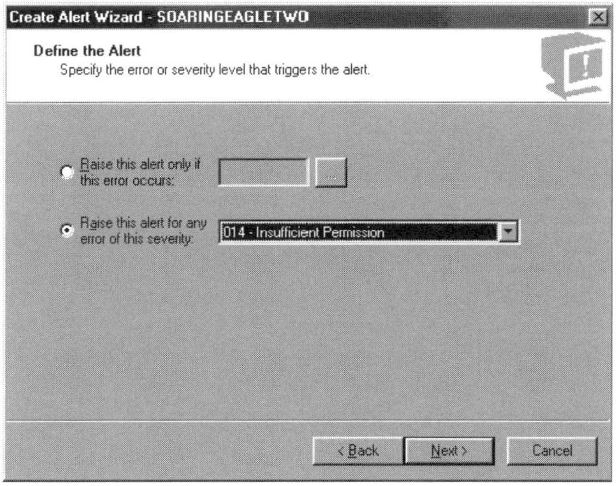

You can choose any database by selecting the drop-down arrow. For this type of alert we have decided that we want to be notified if anyone is trying to get into any of the databases without authorization. We have not put any data in the Error message contains this text box since we want to keep this open to any message. Click **OK**.

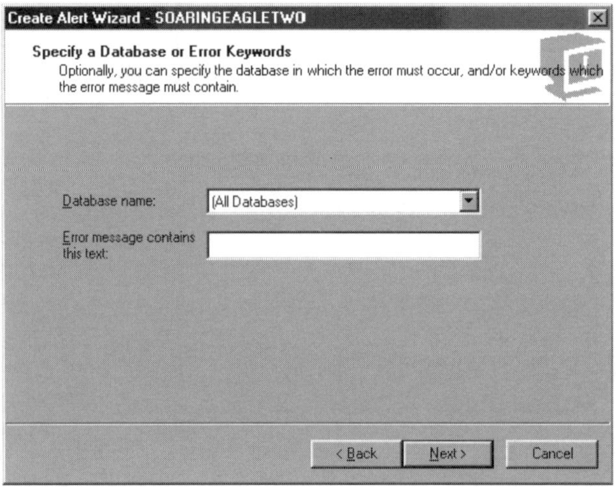

Here you are able to edit the properties of the job you are creating.

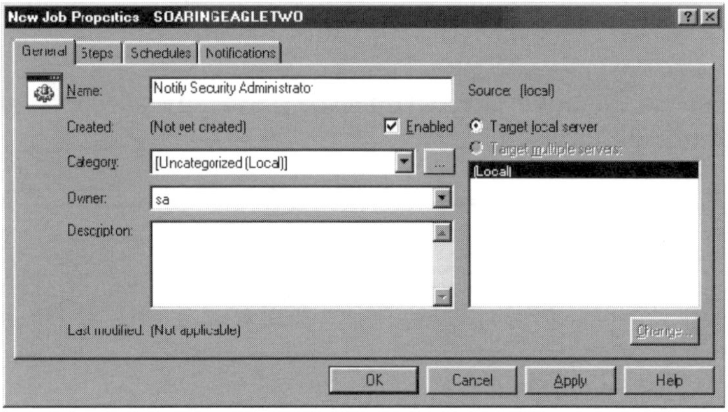

When you get to this screen select **New**.

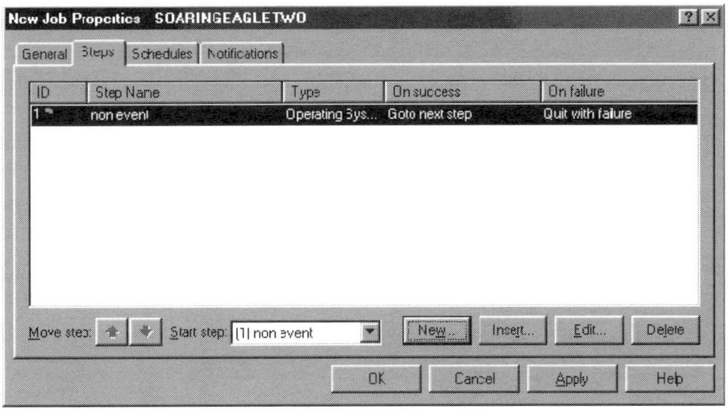

Though you have other options here, all you have to select is the job you wish to execute. Then click **Next**.

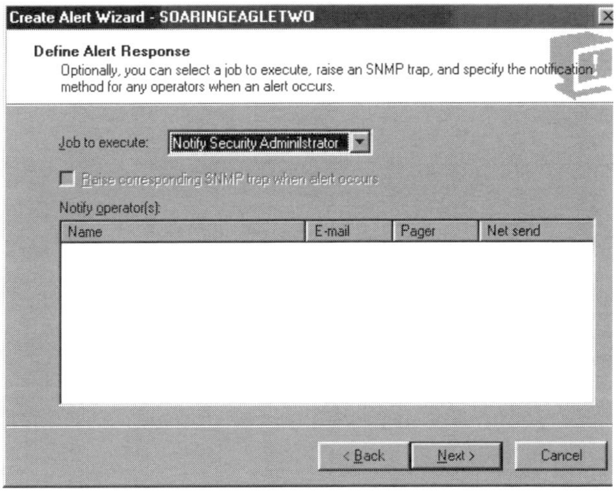

You must have a step but our step is a non-event so set these parameters. The letters cd in the Command box stand for change directory, which is something that will not have any effect on the system. In this case, we are only interested in the end of the job, which is the notification of the administrator. Press **OK**.

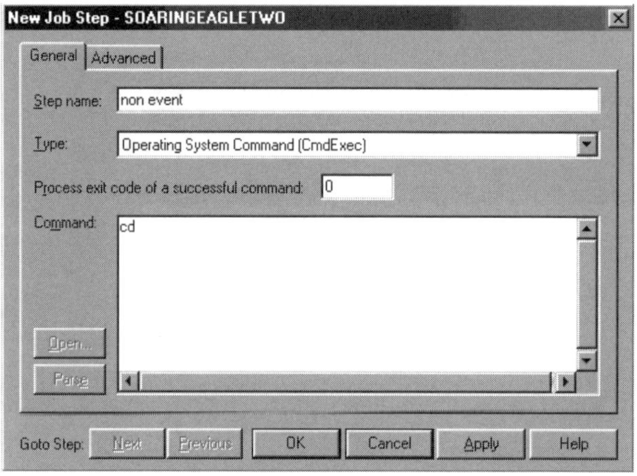

For this particular alert, select the **Notifications** tab. The only automatic process you want to occur is to notify you of an authorized user.

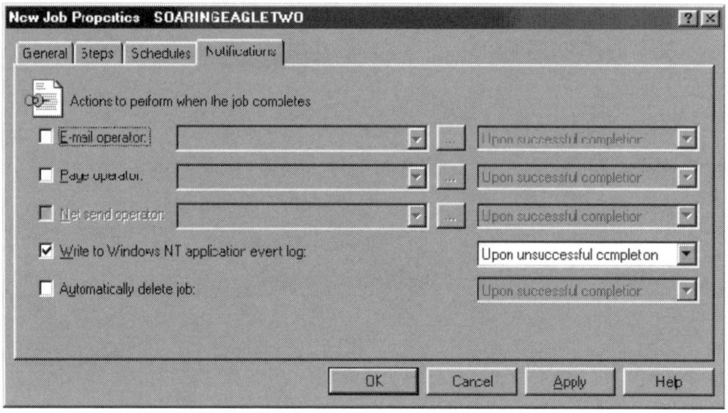

You will get this message if you have not yet defined any operators (people to notify) to the server. Click **Yes**.

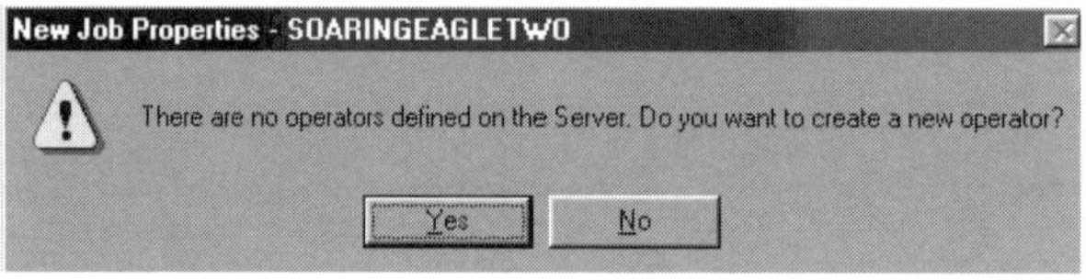

Click **Finish** to confirm your selections.

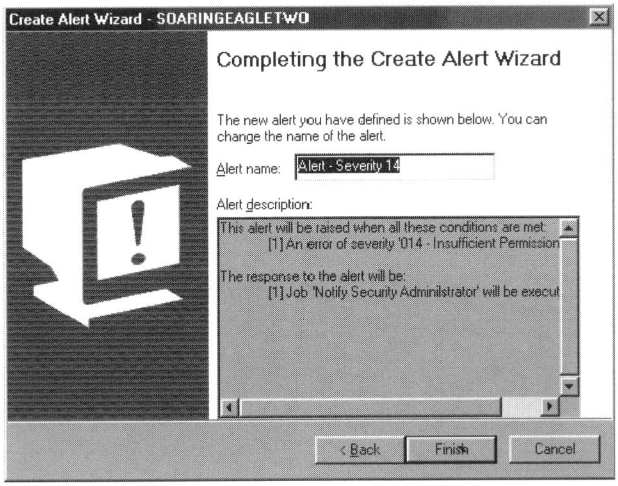

The wizard is complete.

You can see the alert that you have just created by going to the SQL Server Agent. Here you can see all of your alerts, operators, and jobs.

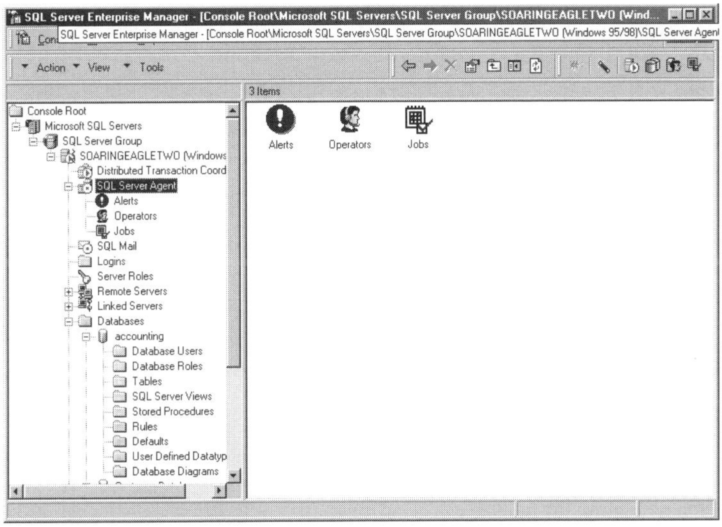

Appendix D

Replication

Sometimes it may be necessary to hold information in more than one place. This can be like keeping copies of your work at home and at the office. However, If you make a change to your work at home, how does the office know what you have done? The same can be true of databases. Sometimes an application may be developed that will require data from other databases. These databases may not even be on the same server but the data will need to exist in more than one database. The data will need to be replicated from one database to the other.

Types of Replication

Replication is the mechanism provided in SQL Server that allows for data and stored procedures to be distributed to other databases. These databases receiving the copied data can be on the same server as the source, or they can exist on other servers. This distribution mechanism also ensures that should the copied data be altered, the change will be reflected throughout the distributed data. In other words, the data will be synchronized so that one copy of the data will match all other copies. Microsoft uses a publish and subscribe model for replication. This model has three key components: the Publisher, the Distributor, and the Subscriber.

The Publisher is the server that provides the data being distributed to other databases. The Distributor is the server with the task of taking the published data and passing it along to all the other servers that require it. The Subscriber is the server that will request information from a Publisher.

Using this model, SQL Server 7.0 supports three types of replication:

- Snapshot replication
- Transactional replication
- Merge replication

Snapshot Replication

Snapshot replication involves taking a "snapshot" of the published data at a particular time. This snapshot is a copy of the schema of the published objects and the data stored in them. A snapshot agent actually takes the snapshot. The snapshot agent will copy the schema and all the data in it. This snapshot is sent to the distribution agent which will send the data to the Subscribers. The Subscribers will not merely receive changes to the data, they will receive a whole new set of data to replace the old data. The old data will be dropped and replaced with the schema and data from the snapshot.

This can be similar to newspaper delivery. A newspaper is prepared at a publisher and distributed by a newspaper carrier to the subscribers. When the subscribers receive the paper, it replaces the newspaper from the previous day.

Transactional Replication

While snapshot replication is a relatively simple form of replication, it can take a lot of time and resources on the server if the tables are very large. This is because snapshot replication forces data to be completely rewritten. An alternative to rewriting entire tables is transactional replication. Transactional replication only distributes the changes to data. If only some rows are modified in a database, then only the modifications are distributed to the Subscribers.

Merge Replication

The third and more complicated form of replication is merge replication. The previous two forms of replication are simple in the sense that the source of the data modifications is the Publisher. However, if other people are using the data in the Subscriber databases, it might be required that a Subscriber be allowed to change the replicated data from a Subscriber server rather than a Publisher. These changes should not only be present in the server where the change was made but also distributed to other subscribing servers.

As an example, we will walk through the steps to set up a snapshot replication environment.

Setting up a Distributor:

1. From the Tools menu, select **Wizards**.
2. Expand the **Replication** option.
3. Select **Configure Publishing and Distribution Wizard**.
4. Click **OK**.

The following figure is an introduction window.

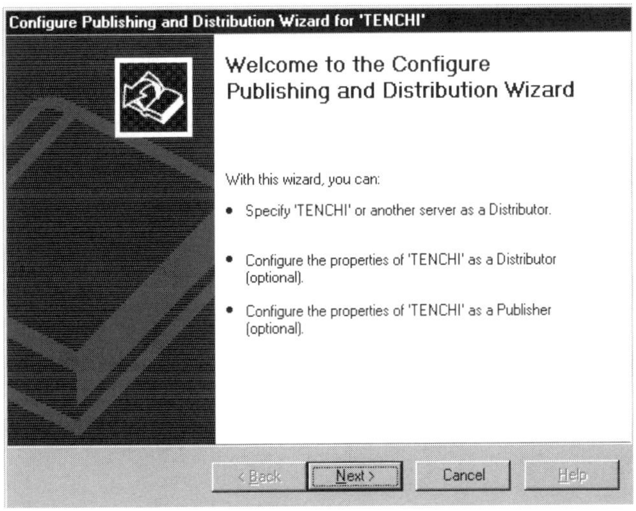

5. Click the **Next** button. The next window asks if the current server is the one being configured as a Distributor. Select **Yes**, to use the local server as a Distributor. (Remote servers can also be used by selecting the No option and choosing a remote server.)

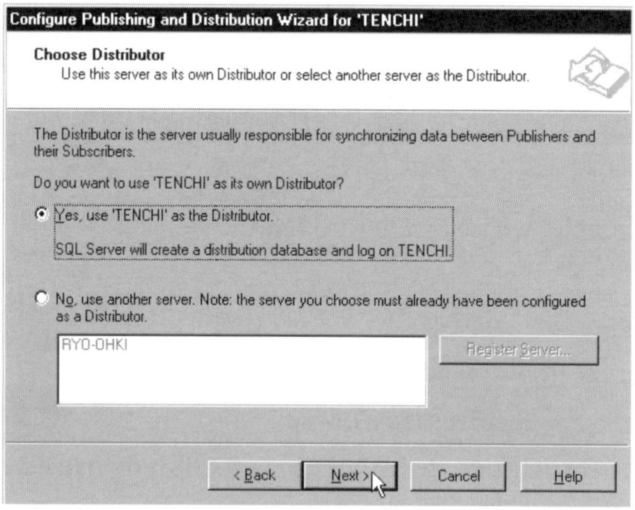

6. Click **Next**. This screen lets you decide whether to use the default distribution settings for SQL Server or customize the distribution settings. The default is to customize.

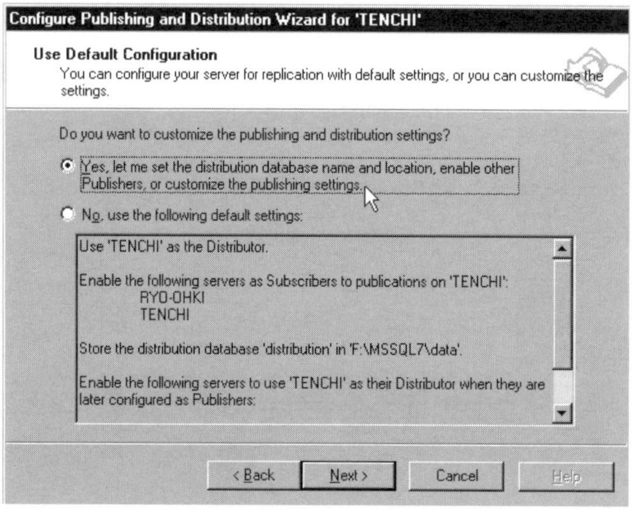

If customize is chosen, the next step is to decide what to name the distribution database and where the distribution database files will be located. Make these selections.

7. Click **Next**. The next piece of information to set is which Publisher servers will be permitted to use this new Distributor. Check any servers that will use the Distributor, then click the button with the ellipsis to set the login and password used to access the server.

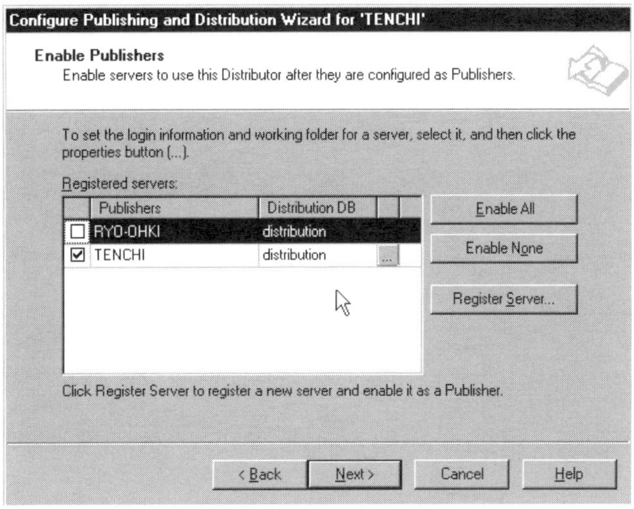

8. Click **Next**. The next step is to select all databases that will be usable as publications from this Distributor. Check Trans for all databases that will be used in transactional or snapshot replication. Also, check Merge for all databases that will be used for merge replication. You may select both.

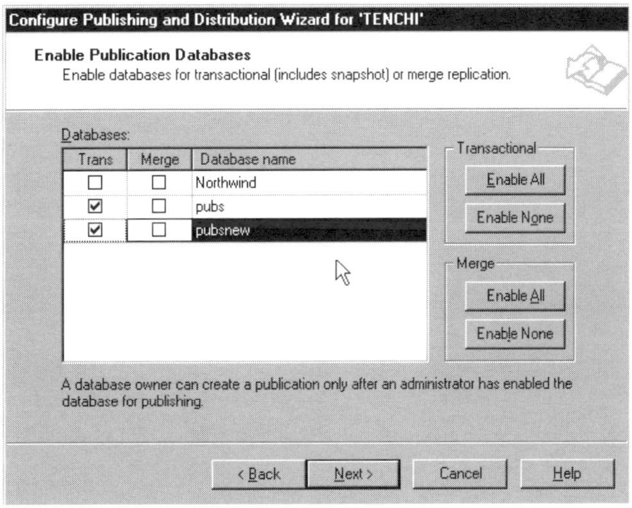

9. Click **Next** to move on. Now you need to decide which Subscriber servers will be allowed to accept publications from this Distributor. Check all servers that can receive from this Distributor and click the button with the ellipsis to set any logins and passwords used to access the server. Now all the distribution options should be set.

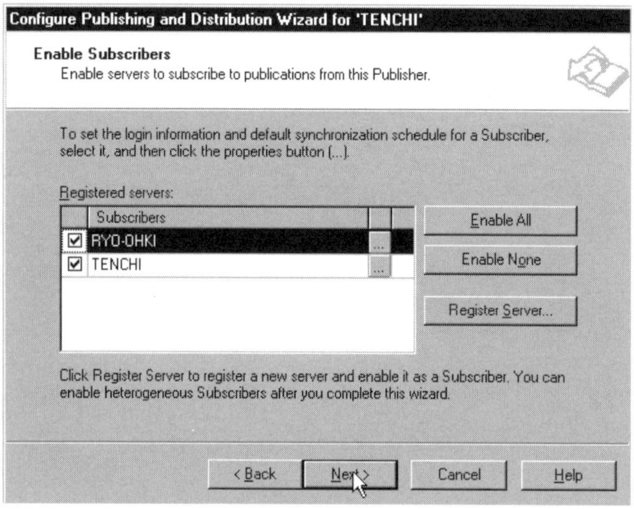

10. Click **Next** to access the final page in the wizard. Click **Finish** to complete setup of the Distributor.

Setting up a Publisher:

1. Select **Wizards** from the Tools menu and choose **Create Publication Wizard**, which is located underneath replication.

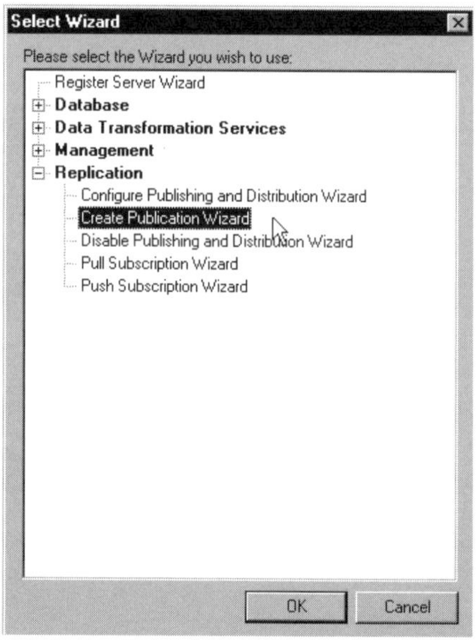

2. Select a database that can be used for publication. Then click the **Create Publication** button.

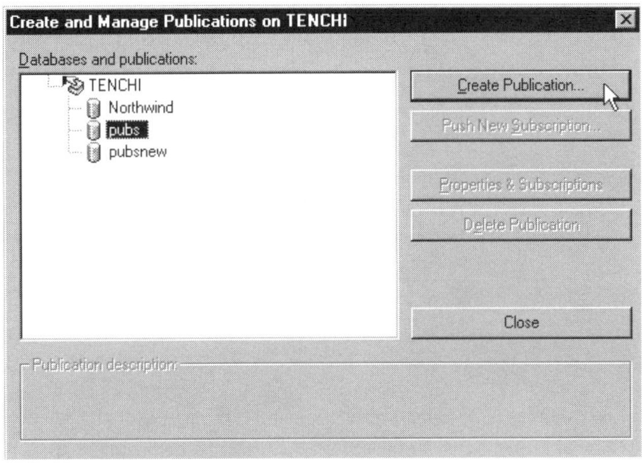

3. This starts the Create Publication Wizard.

4. Click **Next** to move to the first step. Determine if this publication will allow immediate updates to tables or not. Immediate update means that as the Publisher changes the data, the data in the Subscriber databases will be changed immediately. The default is to not allow immediate updates. Since we are setting up a snapshot replication environment, there is no need to change this.

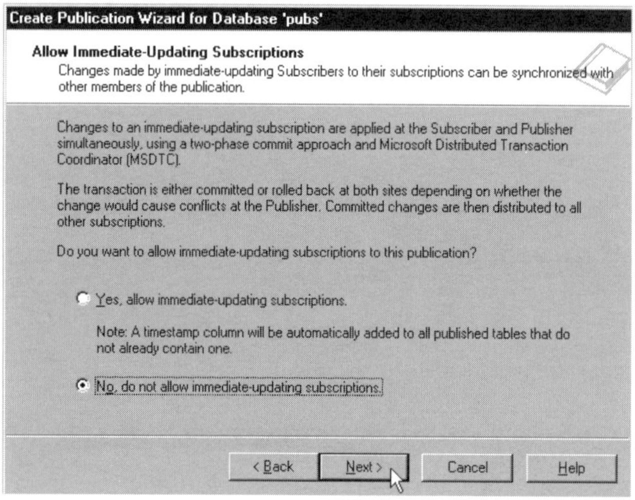

5. Click **Next**. The next step is to configure how replication will communicate to other databases. If all the other database servers are SQL Servers, then choose the default option. If any of the Subscriber databases is not a SQL Server, then the other option must be chosen.

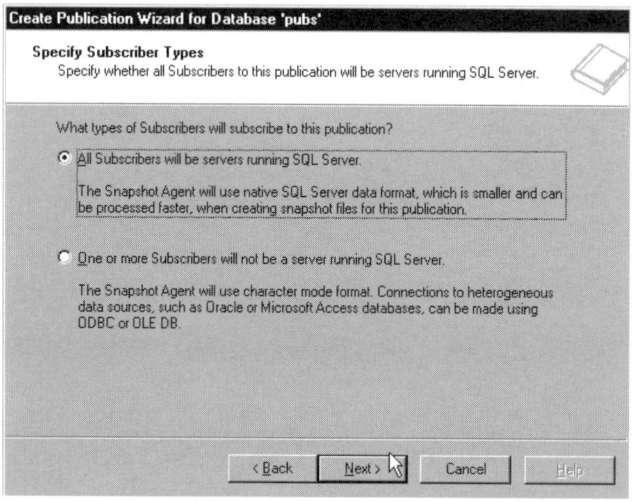

6. Click **Next** to move on. Now you are ready to define the publication. Check any tables that you wish to publish for the publication. By default, SQL Server will provide an article name for each object being published. Clicking the button with the ellipses for the object may change the article name.

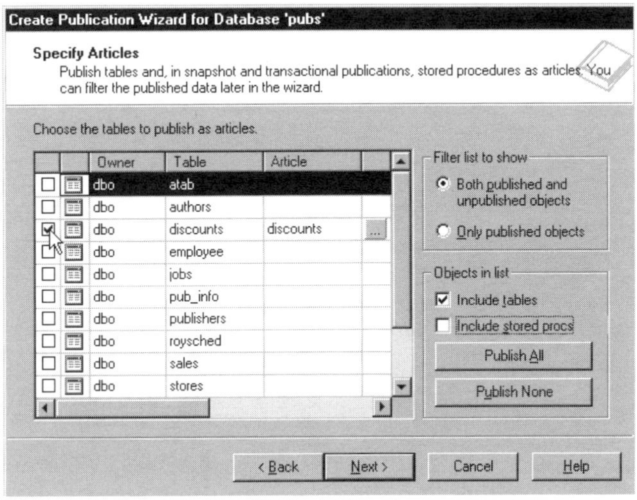

7. Click **Next**. Enter a name and a description for the publication.

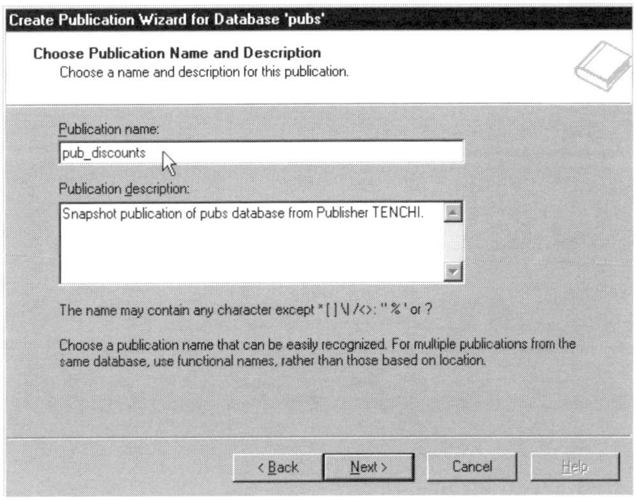

8. Click **Next**. This window will ask if you would like to define any data filters, enable anonymous Subscribers, or customize any other properties. The default is no.

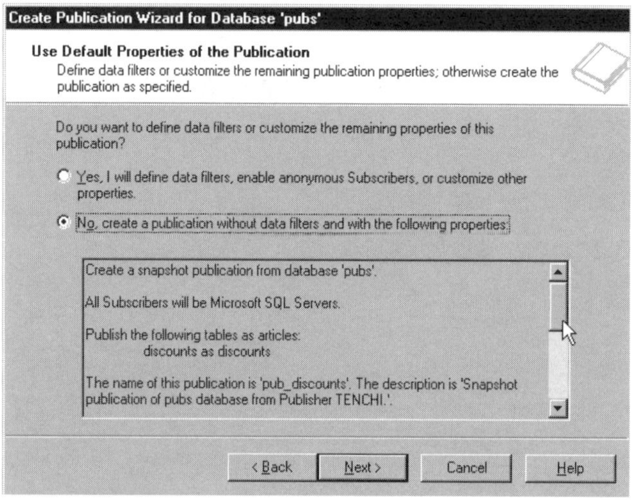

9. Click **Next** to access the final page in the wizard.

10. Click **Finish** to complete the process.

After the publication is created, Enterprise Manager will return to the Create and Manage Publications window from the beginning of the publication process. However, we should now have a publication available. The only thing left to do is create a new subscription to use it. This can be done by clicking the Push New Subscription button, or if you have closed this window, by selecting Tools|Wizards and selecting **Push Subscription Wizard**.

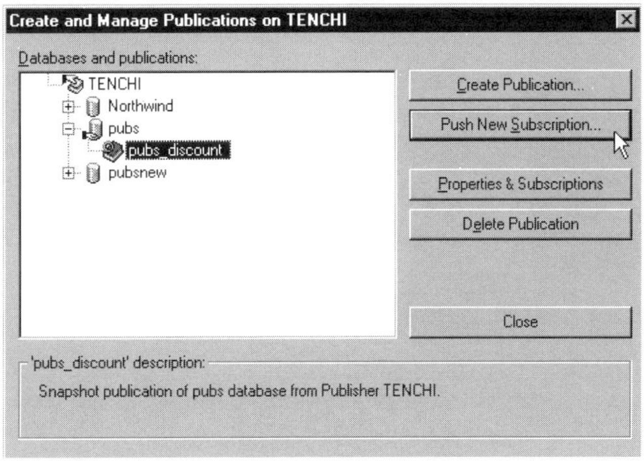

Push vs. Pull

For transactional and merge replication, Subscribers can be defined as *push* or *pull.* Normally Subscribers are push Subscribers. This means that the data transfer was not initiated by the Subscriber. The data are pushed to the Subscriber. Subscribers for snapshot replication are always push Subscribers. A pull subscription is when a Subscriber initiates the data transfer. The Subscriber requests that replicated data be transmitted to the database. The Subscriber is pulling the data from the Distributor.

Setting up a subscription:

1. Select **Tools|Wizards|Push Subscription Wizard**.

2. Click **Next**. Select which server or servers will be used as the Subscriber.

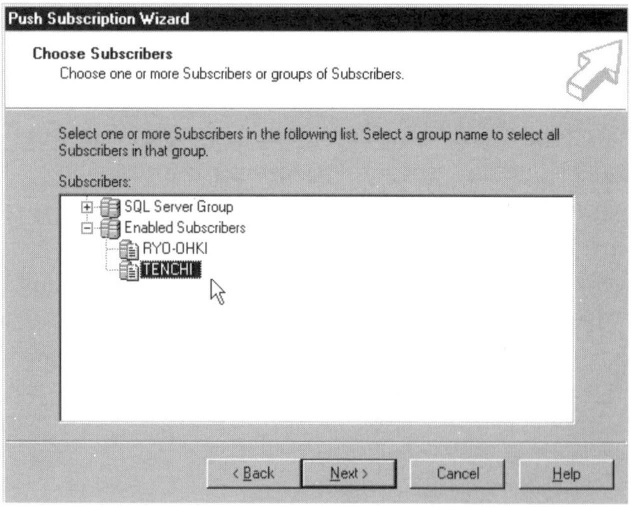

3. Click **Next**. It is required that the database receiving the subscription exist on the server. If the database has a different name, enter the new name in the box or choose from a list of databases by clicking the Browse Databases button.

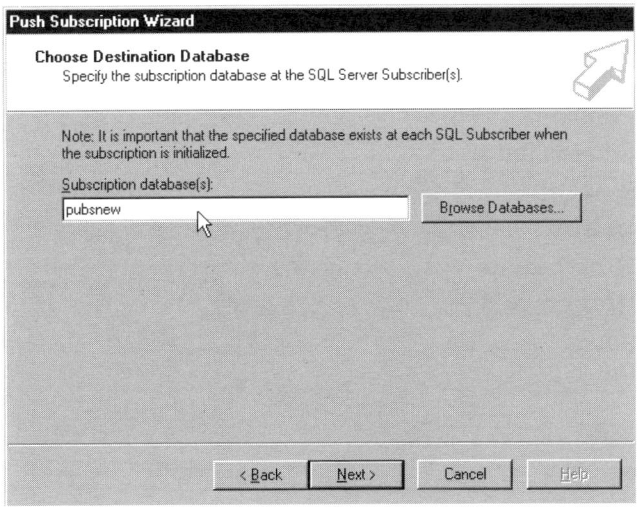

4. The next step is to determine when the Distributor will transmit the data to the Subscriber databases. This can be done continuously or on a schedule. For snapshot replication, continuous transmission is not a good option because the replicated tables would be dropped and re-created any time there was a published change. Therefore, creating a schedule is best. The default schedule is to replicate hourly. (This can be altered by clicking the Change button.)

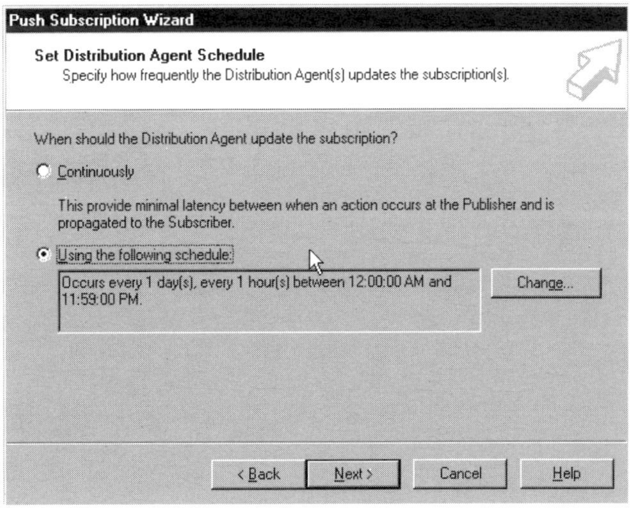

5. Click **Next.** SQL Server needs to know if the Subscriber database needs to have the replicated data and tables build as part of the replication process. If the data already exist, select no. If the data do not exist, select the default yes; this will force SQL Server to use a snapshot agent to take an image of the present published data so it can be replicated to the other databases. It is also recommended to check the **Start the Snapshot Agent** option to start this process as soon as possible.

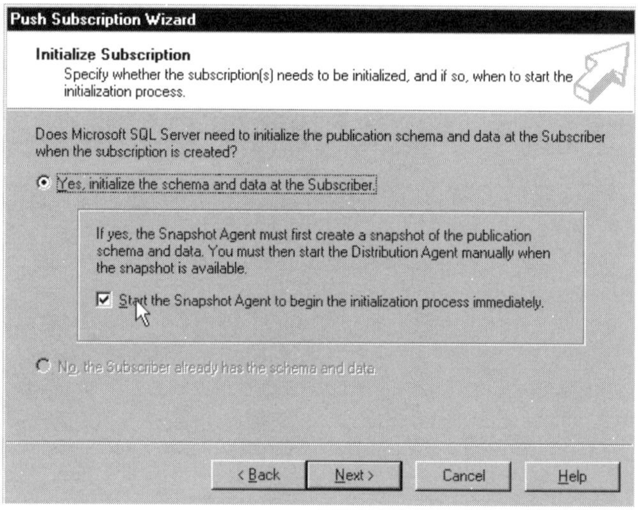

6. Click **Next**. The next step is more of a system check. In order for the replication to work, a SQL Server Agent must be running on the machines involved in replication. Putting a check in front of all the servers in the list will ensure that when the subscription is created the necessary agents will be started as well. If you leave out any required agents, replication will not work until the agents are started.

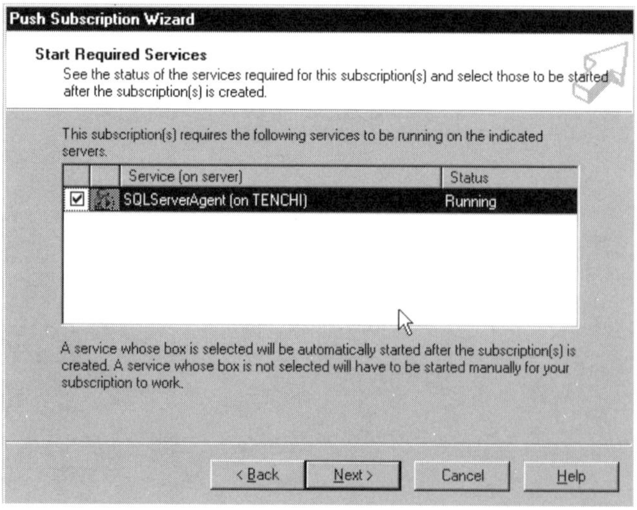

7. Click **Next**. Click **Finish** to complete the process.

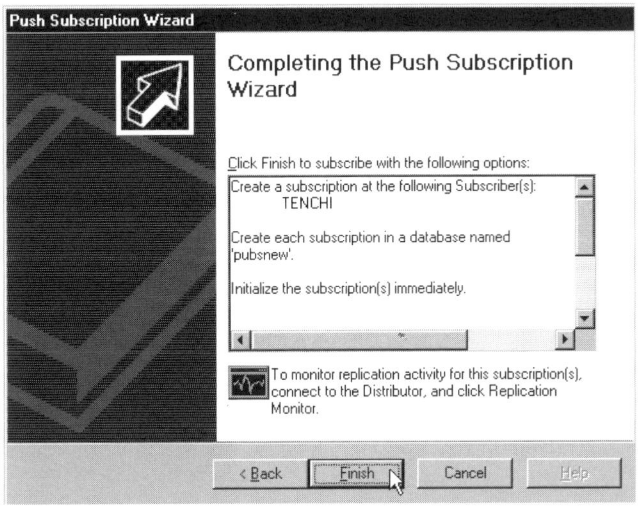

Replication should now be configured. However, it is possible that the data will not be immediately available until the initial snapshot has taken place. This is true of all forms of replication.

Index

A

activity monitoring, 49
Agent, *see* SQL Server Agent
alert, 39, 133
    creating, 133-136
application log, accessing, 65-66

B

backup,
    complete, 84
    differential, 85, 97
backup database command, 84, 96-97
backup device, adding, 93-95
backup media, 84
backup schedule, 87-88
backup storage media, reusing, 20
backup transaction command, 85
backup types, 84-85
Backup Wizard, 170-177
backups, database, *see* database backups
blocking, 143-144
blocking processes,
    eliminating, 53-54
    finding, 52-53
blocking timeout, 144-145

C

client, 1
client/server computing, 1
complete backup, 84
computing, client/server, 1
configuration values, finding, 8-12
Configure Publishing and Distribution Wizard, using, 185-188
cost-based optimizer, 34, 117-118
Create Alert Wizard, 177-181
Create Backup Wizard, *see* Backup Wizard
Create Database Wizard, 156-160
Create Login Wizard, 167-169
Create Publication Wizard, using, 189-192
CREATE STATISTICS, 118

D

data, loss of, 14, 69
database,
    backing up, 88-93, 96-97
    dropping, 102
    expanding size of, 112-114
    monitoring size of, 34, 111-112
    restoring, 18-20, 100-103
database administration, 3
database backup plan, specifying, 163
database backup process, 87-95
database backups, 15, 83
    multiple, 85-86
    performing, 16-17
Database Consistency Checker, *see* DBCC
database dump, 15
Database Maintenance Plan Wizard, 25-26, 160-166
    using, 26-33

database management system, 2
database space, managing, 111-115
database-level maintenance, 14
    automating, 25-33
DBCC, 21, 73
    running, 22-23
DBCC CHECKALLOC, 74-76
DBCC CHECKCATALOG, 74, 76-77
DBCC CHECKDB, 74, 77-78
DBCC CHECKFILEGROUP, 74, 79-81
DBCC commands, 74-81
DBCC DBREINDEX, 128-129
DBCC SHOW_STATISTICS, 118, 124-126
DBMS, *see* database management system
differential backup, 85, 97
disaster recovery, 13-14
disaster recovery plan, 67
disasters,
    potential, 68-69
    recovering from, 70-72
disk mirroring, 68
disk space, 14
Distributor, 183
    setting up, 185-188
DROP STATISTICS, 118

E

Enterprise Manager, 3, 49-50
    using, 3-5
    using for database backup, 88-93
error log, 59
    accessing, 59-61
error log messages, 61-65
error messages, severity level, 63-65
Event Viewer, 65-66

F

fail-over, 68
fragmentation, 36

H

hardware, loss of, 14, 68

I

I/O, configuring, 44
index statistics, updating, 117
Index Tuning Wizard, 38
indexes, 33, 36-37, 127
    creating, 38
    dropping, 37
    rebuilding, 127-128
indexing and upgrade issues, 145-146

J

job, 39, 138
    creating, 138-142
job types, 138

K

keys, 2

L

lock management, 2
locks, 51
    viewing, 51-52
log, viewing, 13

M

maintenance, 7
    database-level, 14
    server-level, 8
    table-level, 33
maintenance tasks, 39-40
master database, 100
memory,
    configuring, 41-43
    overallocated, 146-147
memory configuration parameters, modifying, 47-48
merge replication, 185
messages, monitoring, 13

N

NT Performance Monitor, 55
    accessing, 55

O

operator, 39, 136
    creating, 136-138

P

power, loss of, 14, 69
processes, checking, 50
properties, SQL Server, 8-12
publish and subscribe replication, 183
Publisher, 183
    setting up, 188-193
pull Subscribers, 193
push Subscribers, 193
Push Subscription Wizard, using, 194-197

Q

Query Analyzer,
    opening, 34
    using, 35

R

RDBMS, *see* relational DBMS
reindexing error, 145
relational DBMS, 2
replication, 183
    merge, 185
    publish and subscribe, 183
    snapshot, 184
    transactional, 184
    types of, 184-185
resources, monitoring, 14

S

server, 1-2
    configuring, 45-46
server performance, configuring, 45-48
server-level maintenance, 8
severity level error messages, 63-65
showcontig function, 36
snapshot replication, 184
SP_AUTOSTATS, 118, 121-122
SP_UPDATESTATS, 118, 123
space management, 23-25
spid, 51
SQL Enterprise Manager, *see* Enterprise Manager
SQL Server, 2
    configuring, 41
    installation, 147-149
    loss of, 68-69
    monitoring, 55-57

SQL Server Agent, 131, 142
    configuring, 132-133
    starting, 132
SQL Server version, determining, 149
SQL Server web sites, 153
statistics page, 34
statistics, updating, 34-35
Subscriber, 183-184, 193
subscription, setting up, 194-197
system process ID, *see* spid
systems administration, 2

T

table-level maintenance, 33
tables, 33
    monitoring size of, 34
throughput, maximizing, 45
transaction, 105
transaction log, 20-21, 105-106
    backing up, 21, 97-99
    expanding, 108-110
    full, 149-152
    maintaining, 107-108
    truncating, 106-107
transaction log backup, specifying, 164-165
transaction management, 2
transactional replication, 184

U

uninterruptible power supply, *see* UPS
UPDATE STATISTICS, 118, 119-121
UPS, 14

V

virtual memory, configuring, 46-47

W

Windows NT options, configuring, 45-48
wizard, 155

Other Books from Wordware Publishing, Inc.

Communications/General

The Complete Communications Handbook
Demystifying ATM/ADSL
Demystifying EDI
Demystifying ISDN
Demystifying TCP/IP (3rd Ed.)

Demystifying Virtual Private Networks
Developing Internet Information Services
Digital Imaging in C and the World Wide Web
Learn Advanced Internet Relay Chat
Learn Internet Relay Chat (2nd Ed.)
Learn Microsoft Exchange Server 5.5 Core Technologies
Writing and Publishing with Your PC

Applications/Operating Systems

Learn ACT! 3.0 for Windows 95
Learn ACT! 3.0-4.0 for the Advanced User
Learn ACT! 2000 for the Advanced User
Learn AutoCAD in a Day
Learn AutoCAD 12 in a Day
Learn AutoCAD LT 97 for Windows 95/NT
Learn AutoCAD LT 98
Learn AutoCAD LT 2000
Learn AutoCAD LT 2000 for the Advanced User
Learn AutoCAD LT 2000 for Architects
Learn Linux 3-D Graphics Programming

Applications/Operating Systems

Learn Lotus 1-2-3 Rel. 5 for Windows in a Day
Learn Microsoft Access 2.0 for Windows in a Day
Learn Microsoft Access 7.0 for Windows 95 in a Day

Learn Microsoft Excel 7.0 for Windows 95 in a Day
Learn Microsoft Excel 2000 VBA Programming
Learn Microsoft FrontPage 97
Learn Microsoft Office 95
Learn Microsoft Office 97
Learn Microsoft Office 2000
Learn Microsoft PowerPoint 7.0 for Windows 95 in a Day
Learn Microsoft Publisher 2000 for the Advanced User
Learn Microsoft Word 6.0 for Windows in a Day
Learn Microsoft Word 7.0 for Windows 95 in a Day
Learn Microsoft Works 3.0 for Windows in a Day
Learn Peach Tree Accounting
Learn P-CAD Master Designer
Learn Red Hat Linux OS Tips
Learn Red Hat Linux Server Tips
Learn to Draw with Visio 2000
Learn Visio 5.0

Learn Visio 5.0 for the Advanced User
Learn Visio 2000
Learn Visio 2000 for the Advanced User
Learn Visio 2000 for the Masters
Learn Windows 95 in a Day

Applications/Operating Systems

Learn Word 2000 VBA by Example
Learn Word 2000 VBA Document Automation
Learn WordPerfect 5.2 for Windows in a Day
Learn WordPerfect 6.0 for Windows in a Day
Visio 4 for Everyone
Visio 2000 Developer's Guide: Software Patterns
Windows NT Server 4.0/2000: Testing and Troubleshooting

Programming

Advanced 3-D Game Programming with DirectX 7.0
Collaborative Computing with Delphi 3
CORBA Developer's Guide with XML
Delphi Developer's Guide to OpenGL
Delphi Graphics and Game Programming Exposed! with DirectX

Designing Arcade Computer Game Graphics
Developer's Guide to Computer Game Design
Developer's Guide to Delphi Troubleshooting
Developer's Guide to HP Printers
Developer's Guide to Lotus Notes and Domino R5
Developer's Workshop to COM and ATL 3.0
Developer's Workshop to COM+
Developer's Workshop to COM and Visual Basic 2000
Developing Enterprise Applications with PowerBuilder 6.0
Developing Utilities in Visual Basic 4.0

Programming

The HTML Example Book
Iterative UML Development using Visual Basic 5.0
Iterative UML Development using Visual Basic 6.0
Iterative UML Development using Visual C++ 6.0
Learn ActiveX Development using Visual Basic 5.0
Learn ActiveX Development using Visual C++ 6.0
Learn ActiveX Scripting with Microsoft Internet Explorer 4.0
Learn ActiveX Template Library Development with Visual C++ 6.0
Learn Advanced HTML 4.0 with DHTML

Learn Advanced JavaScript
Learn Advanced JavaScript Programming
Learn C in Three Days
Learn C++ in Three Days
Learn Computer Game Programming with CDX and DirectX 7.0
Learn Computer Game Programming with DirectX 7.0
Learn Encryption Techniques with BASIC and C++
Learn Graphics File Programming with Delphi 3
Learn Microsoft Active Desktop Programming using Windows 98
Learn Microsoft SQL Server 7.0
Learn Microsoft Transaction Server Development using Visual C++ 6.0
Learn Microsoft Visual Basic in Three Days
Learn Object Pascal with Delphi
Learn OLE DB Development with Visual C++ 6.0

Learn Oracle 8i
Learn Pascal
Learn Pascal in Three Days
Learn Personal Oracle 8.0 with Power Objects 2.0
Learn SQL
Learn SQL Server 7.0 Administration
Learn the MFC C++ Classes

Programming

Learn Visual Basic 5.0 in Three Days
Learn Visual C++ in Three Days
Lotus Notes Developer's Guide
Nathan Wallace's Delphi 3 Example Book
Practical Guide to SGML Filters
Practical Guide to SGML/XML Filters

Real-Time Strategy Game Programming using DirectX 6.0
Real-Time Strategy Game Programming using DirectX 7.0
Squirrel's Computer Game Programming in C
Tomes of Delphi: Algorithms and Data Structures

Tomes of Delphi: Win32 Core API—Win 2000 Ed.
Tomes of Delphi: Win32 Database Developer's Guide
Tomes of Delphi: Win32 Graphics Programming
Tomes of Delphi: Win32 Shell API—Win 2000 Ed.

Tomes of Delphi: Win32 Multimedia API
Tomes of Delphi 3: Win32 Core API
Tomes of Delphi 3: Win32 Graphical API
The Visual Basic 4.0 Example Book
The WordBasic Example Book

Networking/Internet

CORBA Networking with Java
DCOM Networking with Visual J++
Learn Internet Publishing with Microsoft Publisher 97
Learn Internet Publishing with Microsoft Publisher 98
Learn Lotus Domino
Practical Guide to Intranet Client-Server Applications using the Web

Let Soaring Eagle Consulting
Carry Your
Database Management Burdens
www.soaringeagleltd.com
888-289-8170